Christian Heroes: Then & Now

LILLIAN TRASHER

The Greatest Wonder in Egypt

CHRISTIAN HEROES: THEN & NOW

LILLIAN TRASHER

The Greatest Wonder in Egypt

JANET & GEOFF BENGE

YWAM Publishing is the publishing ministry of Youth With A Mission (YWAM), an international missionary organization of Christians from many denominations dedicated to presenting Jesus Christ to this generation. To this end, YWAM has focused its efforts in three main areas: (1) training and equipping believers for their part in fulfilling the Great Commission (Matthew 28:19), (2) personal evangelism, and relief work).

To learn more about our books and materials, call (425) 771-1153 or (800) 922-2143 or email books@ywampublishing.com. Visit us online at www.ywampublishing.com.

Lillian Trasher: The Greatest Wonder in Egypt
Copyright © 2004 by YWAM Publishing

Published by YWAM Publishing
a ministry of Youth With A Mission
P.O. Box 55787, Seattle, WA 98155

All rights reserved. No part of this book may be reproduced in any form without permission in writing from the publisher, except in the case of brief quotations in critical articles or reviews.

Library of Congress Cataloging-in-Publication Data
Benge, Janet, 1958–
 Lillian Trasher : the greatest wonder in Egypt / by Janet and Geoff Benge.
   p. cm. — (Christian heroes, then & now)
 Includes bibliographical references (p.   ).
 ISBN 978-1-57658-305-0
 1. Trasher, Lillian Hunt, 1887¬–1961—Juvenile literature. 2. Women missionaries—Egypt—Asyâuòt—Biography—Juvenile literature.
3. Orphanages—Egypt—Asyâuòt—Juvenile literature. [1. Trasher, Lillian Hunt, 1887–1961. 2. Missionaries. 3. Women—Biography. 4. Orphanages—Egypt—Asyâuòt.] I. Benge, Geoff, 1954– II. Title. III. Series.
 BV3572.T7B46 2004
 266'.0092—dc22   2003022068

ISBN 978-1-57658-305-0 (paperback)
ISBN 978-1-57658-596-2 (e-book)

Seventh printing 2025

Printed in the United States of America

CHRISTIAN HEROES: THEN & NOW

- Adoniram Judson
- Albert Schweitzer
- Amy Carmichael
- Betty Greene
- Brother Andrew
- Cameron Townsend
- Charles Mulli
- Clarence Jones
- Corrie ten Boom
- Count Zinzendorf
- C. S. Lewis
- C. T. Studd
- David Bussau
- David Livingstone
- Dietrich Bonhoeffer
- D. L. Moody
- Elisabeth Elliot
- Eric Liddell
- Florence Young
- Francis Asbury
- George Müller
- Gladys Aylward
- Helen Roseveare
- Hudson Taylor
- Ida Scudder
- Isobel Kuhn
- Jacob DeShazer
- Jim Elliot
- John Flynn
- John Newton
- John Wesley
- John Williams
- Jonathan Goforth
- Klaus-Dieter John
- Lillian Trasher
- Loren Cunningham
- Lottie Moon
- Mary Slessor
- Mildred Cable
- Nate Saint
- Norman Grubb
- Paul Brand
- Rachel Saint
- Richard Wurmbrand
- Rowland Bingham
- Samuel Zwemer
- Sundar Singh
- Wilfred Grenfell
- William Booth
- William Carey

Available in paperback, e-book, and audiobook formats. Unit study curriculum guides are available for select biographies.

www.YWAMpublishing.com

The authors would like to thank
the Assemblies of God World Missions
in Springfield, Missouri,
for their help in writing this book.

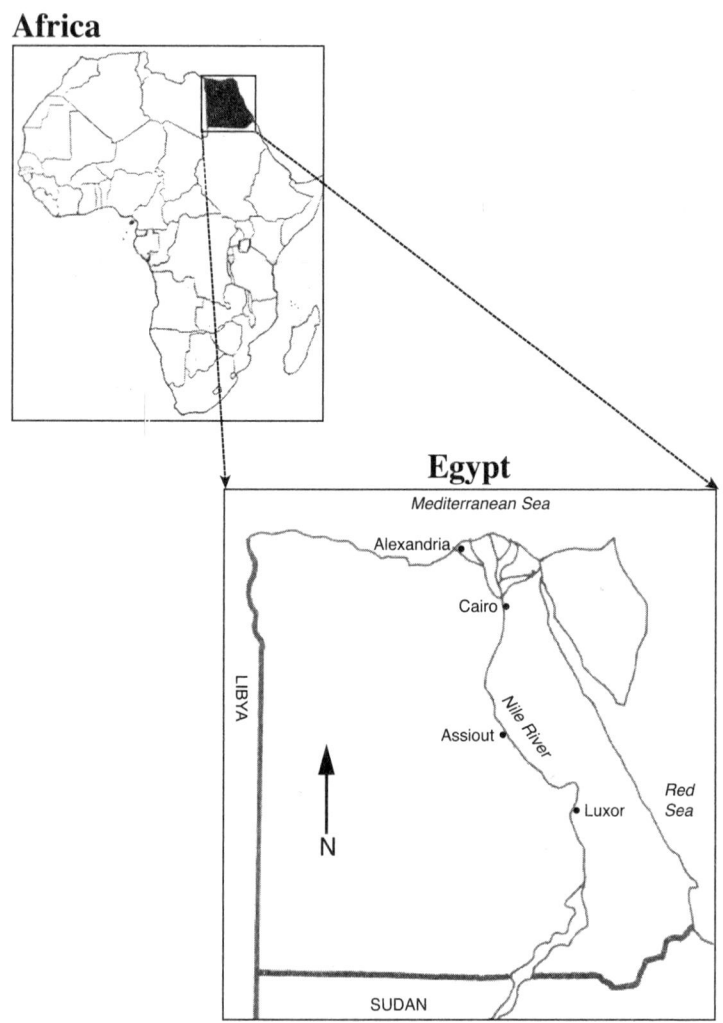

Contents

1. Danger in the Darkness 11
2. Searching for Something 17
3. Something Better 27
4. A Real, Live Missionary 39
5. Assiout 51
6. Fareida 61
7. Plague 73
8. Land Across the Nile 83
9. Bricks 93
10. Losses and Gains 101
11. Rebellion 111
12. A Sad Goodbye 119
13. Unexpected Blessings 131
14. Blessing and Loss 141
15. Holes in the Desert 155
16. A Shipload of Supplies 165
17. "I Stayed with the Work God Gave Me to Do" 179
    Bibliography 190

Chapter 1

Danger in the Darkness

Lillian Trasher counted heads one more time, gasping as she placed her hand on the head of the last child. *How could it be?* she agonized. Two of the toddlers were missing! Her heart thumped as she realized they must have been left behind.

"I must go and rescue the two missing children. Make sure everyone stays in here," Lillian said as she turned to Wadeah, one of her older girls. "And don't let anyone in. I'll knock three times when I get back."

"Get back?" wailed the teenager. "Mama, you can't go out there. You'll be killed. Please stay here. What will we do without you?"

"God will protect me. I must go—I must rescue my babies," Lillian said as she gathered up her skirt. "Pray for me and for the babies—they mustn't make a sound."

Lillian paused when she reached the door of the old brick kiln in which she was hiding with the 107 children from her orphanage. Bang! Bang! Two bullets hit the bricks outside as she hesitated. She waited another thirty seconds. She heard yelling in the distance and then more gunfire.

Now is my chance, Lillian told herself. *God, help me to find the children and get back alive,* she prayed as she drew the bolt on the door and slipped outside.

It was a moonlit night, one she would normally have enjoyed. Tonight, however, in Assiout, Egypt, in 1919, every shadow seemed ominous, every cracking twig a threat. Lillian inched her way noiselessly toward the main dormitory building.

How could they have been left behind? she wondered as she crept along. Each child in the orphanage had an older girl who watched over the younger child, and Lillian insisted the children practice emergency drills once a month. Now, when it really mattered, something had gone wrong. One of the girls must have panicked and simply run for her life. Lillian could not blame her. It was one thing to practice a drill but quite another to see strange men, rifles cocked, storming the gates of your home. The school bell had rung, and the children, widows, and staff had less than two minutes to run for the old brick kiln, the closest secure structure to the orphanage.

What's done is done, Lillian said to herself as she fumbled for the keys to the door. She looked out across the Nile River to Assiout, where parts of the city were ablaze. Orange flames reflected off the surface of the river, making it appear to be on fire as well. Just then the key turned in the lock, and Lillian breathed a quick prayer as she ran in: *God, help me find the missing children before the intruders do.*

Inside the orphanage Lillian raced upstairs, flinging open each door and frantically searching rooms for signs of life. Finally she spotted them—two little girls huddled in the corner of a crib, whimpering. "Shhhhh," Lillian said as she scooped up one girl in each arm and sprinted for the door. "Mama needs you to be very quiet," she told them as she locked the door behind her and took a deep breath. Now she had to make it safely back to the brick kiln, this time carrying two toddlers. She adjusted the weight of the children on her hips and began running.

A cloud was now covering the moon, and the night sky was pitch black. Lillian breathed a sigh of relief. The intruders might have guns, but Lillian had an advantage over them because she knew every inch of the property in light and darkness.

About fifty yards from the building, Lillian's blood froze. She heard someone yelling after her, "Stop! Stop!" Lillian kept running.

"English, English," the man called this time. "Over here."

Lillian heard another shout in the darkness and then the sound of running feet.

Crack. Lillian felt a burst of hot air near her right ear. Her hands shook as she realized it must have been a bullet. They were shooting at her! Instinctively she dived for the ground, trying to protect the toddlers from the impact. As Lillian rolled sideways into a shallow irrigation ditch, a searing pain stabbed her ankle. She had twisted it. Pushing all thoughts of the pain aside, Lillian turned her attention to the children. Gently she placed a hand over each child's mouth to let the children know they must keep quiet. One sound now and they would be discovered and shot. She silently thanked God for the irrigation ditch, which provided cover from the bullets and gave them a place to hide.

Every sense in Lillian's body was alert as she lay in the ditch. Two sets of footsteps marched closer, stopping about ten yards from her. "She has to be here somewhere," a voice said in Arabic.

"I hope I am the one to shoot her," a second voice interjected. "Egypt does not need meddling Englishwomen!" Lillian heard him spit on the ground.

These men from the north think I'm English! Lillian thought as a chill ran down her spine. Egypt was rebelling against their British overlords, trying to rid the land of everything English. But Lillian was not English; she was an American. The Egyptians had nothing against Americans, but so much hatred had been stirred up in the past several months that these Egyptian men might kill anyone who was a foreigner.

The little girl in Lillian's right arm whimpered, and the men stopped talking. Lillian held her breath and wiggled still farther down into the bottom of the irrigation ditch. She was afraid the men would hear the loud beating of her heart.

Just then a booming voice called to the two men. "Everyone over here." The men hesitated for a moment and then slung their rifles over their shoulders and walked away. Lillian held her breath as the sound of the men's footsteps receded. The men were heading away from the kiln toward the Nile River.

Lillian let out a sigh of relief. She waited a full minute after the men had disappeared completely into the darkness before she took her hands away from the children's mouths. She clambered out of the irrigation ditch and set out for the old brick kiln as quickly as she could. Her twisted ankle sent bolts of pain all the way up her right side, but Lillian willed herself forward. Within minutes she was safely inside the thick walls of the old kiln, surrounded by all her children, who were relieved and delighted at her safe return.

As she caught her breath, Lillian wondered what her friends back home in the United States would think if they could see her now. True, she had told them she was coming to serve the Egyptian people, but she never imagined that one day she would be dodging bullets and willingly risking her own life to save two orphan children. Nothing in her childhood or teenage years had given Lillian any hint of the adventurous life that lay ahead.

Chapter 2

Searching for Something

"May I sit here?" seventeen-year-old Lillian Trasher asked, eyeing the window seat midway down the train carriage.

"Of course, my dear," replied the middle-aged woman sitting in the aisle seat. "Are you traveling alone?"

Lillian nodded. It was her first big adventure away from her family, and she intended to savor every moment of it.

Lillian settled her canvas bag on her lap. Packed in it were her pencils and sketches, sketches that she hoped would land her a job at Atlanta's *Georgian* newspaper. Lillian took a deep breath and stretched out her long legs. Her toes already felt cramped in the new shoes her father had bought her for the trip.

Soon the train hissed and the conductor yelled, "All aboard." Lillian pulled the window down and peered out, hoping to catch a glimpse of her mother and father. There they were among the crowd. For a second Lillian felt sorry for them. She had only one sibling, a sister named Jennie, who had already moved west to Long Beach, California. Jennie was a stenographer and had made enough money there to buy herself a small house by the ocean. Now Lillian was setting out to make her own way in the world, and it would be just her parents left living in Asheville, North Carolina.

Lillian spotted her mother waving a handkerchief as the train pulled slowly away from the station. Lillian was finally on her way.

As the train gathered steam, Lillian thought about the weeks that lay ahead. She was taking the train first to Brunswick, at the southeast tip of Georgia, to visit some old friends. Until a year ago, Lillian and her family had lived in Brunswick. Then her father moved the family to Asheville to get a better job. From Brunswick she would head northwest to Atlanta to apply for a job as a sketch artist for the *Georgian*. So many good things were happening to Lillian all at once that she could hardly believe it. *Just think,* she told herself, *three months from now, I could be an independent working girl with money for hats and jewelry. Why, I might even save up enough to take a train trip out to California.*

"Where are you headed?" a voice asked, breaking through Lillian's thoughts.

Lillian turned to the woman sitting beside her. The woman had a Bible open on her lap. Lillian smiled at her. "I'm off to Brunswick for a visit and then on to Atlanta, where I hope to settle down."

"Are you getting married there?" the woman inquired.

"Oh, no!" Lillian exclaimed. "I'm hoping to get a job working for a newspaper."

"My, my," the woman said, shaking her head. "I suppose it is 1905, but the thought of young girls off on their own with jobs... Do you think you can manage?"

"I expect so," Lillian replied. "I've been drawing things for as long as I can remember, and my mother has a friend in Atlanta that I can stay with while I get settled." She paused for a moment. "By the way, my name is Lillian Trasher."

"Of course. I forgot to introduce myself. I am Mattie Perry, *Miss* Mattie Perry, though you wouldn't know it by the number of children I have at home."

"Pleased to meet you, Miss Perry. How many children do you have?"

Mattie laughed. "Last count it was one hundred, but the Lord brings in more all the time. I run the Faith Orphanage in Marion, North Carolina. Have you heard of it?"

"No, I haven't," Lillian replied. "Tell me about it."

Mattie closed her Bible, tucked it in her handbag, and sat back. "Well, it's one of those stories that's hard to tell. No two days are ever the same. I run the orphanage, but the Lord supplies all our needs."

"What do you mean by that?" Lillian asked.

"It's simple, really. I don't have time to go out and raise money while taking care of the needs of that many children, so we pray, and the Lord sends in money and provisions. He hasn't failed me yet. I don't have money to buy food for tomorrow night's supper, but it will come." Mattie fixed her piercing, brown eyes on Lillian. "It's about living by faith, child. There is no end to what you can do if you follow God's call and trust Him to take care of the rest. Do you know the Lord?"

"Yes, I do," Lillian said. "I accepted Jesus into my heart at a prayer meeting at our neighbors'. In fact, they are the people I am going to stay with in Brunswick. You would love Anna Mason. She talks like you, about trusting God and things like that."

"I don't believe things happen to the Lord's children by chance, do you?" Mattie did not wait for an answer. "I think that we were meant to sit together and that I was meant to tell you about the orphanage. In fact, I am badly in need of an assistant. Why don't you come and live with me and help with the children? You could study the Bible in your spare time."

Lillian looked out the window. What could she say? She had known this woman for only ten minutes, and now the woman was inviting her to change her life plans and work in an orphanage! Lillian wanted to laugh out loud, but she was too well brought up to do so. Instead she replied, "Thank you for the offer. I'll think about it."

"Sometimes thinking isn't the right thing to do," Mattie replied. "Ask the Lord to direct your steps; that's all you have to do."

"I suppose you're right," Lillian said, glad that the train was pulling into a station.

Mattie gathered up her handbag and stood up. "I have to get off here. I'm on my way to collect a child whose mother died of fever in the spring and whose father can't cope any longer." She reached down and patted Lillian's hand. "You remember my offer, dear. It's the Faith Orphanage in Marion, North Carolina," she said. "Stranger things have happened. I will be praying for you."

"Thank you," Lillian mumbled. "I'll remember, the Faith Orphanage in Marion, North Carolina."

No one took Mattie's seat, and so Lillian was left alone with her thoughts. Mattie's words, "There is no end to what you can do if you follow God's call and trust Him to take care of the rest," kept echoing in her mind as cows and trees appeared to whisk by the carriage window. The words made Lillian uneasy. *I do often feel like something is missing in my life—but I already have my life mapped out,* she told herself. *God gave me the talent to draw. Surely He expects me to use it. When I get to Atlanta, I'll go to church every Sunday, and when things settle down, I'll even offer to teach a Sunday-school class.*

Now that Lillian had things worked out in her mind, she pulled a sketchpad and pencil from her bag and started drawing the interior of the train carriage.

After many hours of rolling through the Georgia countryside, the train steamed into the Brunswick station. Lillian recognized her old neighbor Ed Mason waiting for her. Beside Ed stood a young woman. Lillian peered at her and then laughed out loud. It was her old friend Jerdy! How she had grown in the year they had been apart. Lillian hardly recognized her. Suddenly Lillian felt self-conscious. She had grown as well, to six feet tall, and now that her mother let her wear her long, brown hair piled up on her head instead of in braids, she knew she looked even taller. Picking up her bag, Lillian exited the train. Her nervousness was gone the instant she heard Jerdy's voice. They might be young women now, but they shared a wealth of childhood memories from growing up together.

Lillian's luggage was unloaded from the boxcar and hoisted up onto the old cart she remembered so well. As the horses clipped along the dirt road to the Masons' cottage, Lillian's mind played over all the reasons she had loved living in Brunswick. There were the creek where she bathed every day in summer, the plump blackberries she and Jerdy picked for pie filling, and Daisy, the world's boniest horse, who had patiently carried them across the cotton fields. Lillian knew that her family had not always lived in Georgia. She had vague memories of Boston, where the family had lived in luxury until something happened to the family finances and they moved south to the small farm cottage in Brunswick. Before Boston the Trasher family had lived briefly in the South, but Lillian had no memory of it. All she knew was that she had been born in Jacksonville, Florida.

As the cart rounded a corner, Lillian saw the old tree where she and Jerdy had made many secret forts.

"We're here!" Jerdy yelled.

Jerdy's mother, Anna Mason, hurried out of the cottage. She was engulfed as usual by some of Jerdy's six younger brothers and sisters. Still, she had a broad smile on her face as she wiped her hands on her apron. "Just in time for supper, honey!" she said as she helped Lillian down from the cart and locked her in an embrace.

Inside the farmhouse the familiar aroma of bacon and homemade soap permeated the air. It was good to be back among the Masons again.

The week at the Mason house sped by. Lillian loved being part of a large, rambunctious family again, and she especially loved the times she spent with Anna Mason. Lillian's family was Catholic, but as a child Lillian had not felt the freedom to talk about spiritual things with her parents. She was drawn to Anna's openness about her faith.

The day before Lillian was due to leave, she found herself alone with Anna. The younger children were at school, and Jerdy had gone into town with her father to buy some seed.

"May I talk to you about something?" Lillian asked, feeling strangely shy.

"Sure you can," Anna replied.

Lillian hesitated for a moment and then began. "I don't know how to describe my problem, if it *is* a problem," she started. "I feel like I am searching for something but it's just out of my reach. And I don't know what it is that I am searching for. It just seems like something is missing in my life."

"Umm," Anna mused. "It's not easy to be looking for something when you don't know what it is you're looking for. I wish I could give you some direction, but all I can say is keep praying, and I will pray for you too. Somehow I get the feeling what you want is not far away."

"So do I," Lillian agreed, "but sometimes I think I'll never find it."

"You will, honey, you will," Anna said. "Just keep close to God, and He'll show it to you."

Later that day Lillian took a long walk through the woods. She felt less restless after her talk with Anna. Even though she was no closer to finding out what was missing in her life, she knew she was in God's hands.

The smell of the pine trees and the scampering of squirrels took Lillian back to the hundreds of times she had walked the path between her family's cottage and the Masons' house. About twenty minutes into her walk, she came upon a fallen tree that blocked the path. Lillian stood and stared at it. Could it really be six years since she had stopped at this very tree and knelt down to pray? Looking back, it seemed a strange thing to do, but at the time it made perfect sense. At that time she had been to several prayer meetings at the Mason house, and although she did not have the confidence to pray or speak out loud, something about the meetings attracted her. She started to read one of her mother's Bibles, and it was at this fallen tree where she first knelt to pray. Lillian smiled to herself as she recalled every word of her prayer. Then suddenly she felt the urge to kneel and pray there once again.

Lillian slipped to her knees on the mossy path and repeated once again her first prayer. "Lord, I want to be Your girl. If ever I can do anything for You, just let me know and—and I'll do it." Tears trickled down her cheeks as she spoke the words. Then Lillian added, "I still mean it."

Chapter 3

Something Better

Lillian stood at the trolley stop on Confederate Avenue in Atlanta and watched the carriages and horses clop by. It was a windy afternoon, so with one gloved hand she gripped her sketch bag tightly while she held her hat on her head with the other.

With the jingle of a bell, a trolley car slid to a halt in front of Lillian. It was an electric trolley, the first she had ever ridden in. As she climbed aboard, Lillian decided she liked electricity. Unlike the steam train she had ridden the day before from Brunswick, the electric trolley was quiet and clean.

Within minutes Lillian was whisked into the heart of downtown Atlanta, where her hostess had drawn a map of how to navigate the two blocks from the trolley stop to the newspaper office. Lillian found the place without any difficulty. She took a deep breath before opening the double oak doors and walking into the world she hoped to inhabit.

Lillian had never actually been inside a newspaper office before, and she was surprised to find that it was noisier inside than out on the street. Everyone sat in a single, large room. Partitions divided the room, but they barely reached four feet high, and Lillian could easily see over them and take in everything that was happening in the place. Six women sat typing furiously. The clicking of the keys of their typewriters reminded Lillian of the chickens pecking at the Mason farm. Two young boys walked briskly around the room, dropping papers into wire baskets on various desks and retrieving papers from other wire baskets. At the back of the room, two men, sitting in a haze of tobacco smoke, were engaged in some kind of lively debate.

While it was not the sort of place Lillian had been before, she loved the atmosphere from the moment she walked in. Everyone was intent on his or her work, and so much was going on that it made Lillian feel alive.

After taking in the scene, Lillian walked up to the reception desk and asked to see Mr. Howard, the art editor. Mr. Howard turned out to be one of the men engaged in the animated discussion. He beckoned Lillian into a small office with large, glass windows that overlooked the room. When he had closed the door, the noise of the room outside was only slightly muffled.

"So, you are Miss Lillian Trasher," Mr. Howard said in a southern drawl. "I have been looking forward to meeting you. I take it you have a portfolio to show me."

Nervously Lillian reached for her sketch bag and pulled out twelve of her prize sketches. "Yes, sir," she replied, offering the editor the sketches.

Mr. Howard leaned forward and took them from her. He flicked through the sketches, and Lillian watched as his eyebrows raised.

"Quite impressive," he finally said. "I'd like to take a longer look at them right now, but I have a five o'clock deadline and a splitting headache. Leave the sketches with me and come back at ten o'clock tomorrow. I'll be able to tell you then if you have the job or not. But looking at your work quickly as I have, I'd say there's a good chance you will." He got up and opened the door, and Lillian gathered her things and walked out.

The interview had been much shorter than Lillian imagined it would be, and much more successful too. Lillian was sure Mr. Howard had been impressed with her work, and she was equally sure she would love working in the hustle and bustle of a newspaper office.

The following morning Lillian was up bright and early. She decided to do a little window shopping before heading to the newspaper office. Several dress shops in Atlanta were reputed to carry reproductions of the latest French fashions, which Lillian was eager to see.

When ten o'clock came, Lillian was standing right outside the office of the *Georgian*. As she entered the busy newsroom, she did not see Mr. Howard anywhere. Another man was sitting in the windowed office.

"Is Mr. Howard in?" Lillian asked anxiously.

"I'm afraid not," the receptionist replied, barely taking her eyes off the pages she was sorting. "He's laid up with the flu. Mr. Whiting's covering his work. Do you want to talk to him?"

"I suppose that would be best," Lillian replied. "Is he the one in the office?"

"That's him," the receptionist said.

Lillian made her way through the maze of activity to the back of the newsroom. She knocked on the office door, and Mr. Whiting invited her in.

"I've come about the position as a sketch artist," Lillian said, getting right to the point. "I left some sketches with Mr. Howard yesterday, and he said to come back today and he'd tell me whether or not I have the job."

"Oh," Mr. Whiting said, throwing up his hands, "you have to be the fifth person to come in so far. Look, I don't know what to tell you except that Mr. Howard found someone he said was outstanding for the job, and he has given it to that person. I guess it wasn't your lucky day."

Lillian sat quietly trying to take in the words that had unraveled her exciting future.

"May I have my sketches back then, please?" she managed to ask.

Mr. Whiting rummaged around on the desk, lifting papers and moving newspaper pages.

"I can't find a darn thing here," he said, raising his hands helplessly again. "Someone else wanted his drawings back this morning, and I couldn't find them either. I'll tell you what. Come back in two or three days. Mr. Howard will be back then, and he'll be able to lay his hands on them, I'm sure."

Lillian looked around the room. She had to admit it was a daunting task to find her sketches among the piles of papers that choked the office.

"Thank you," she mumbled as she left.

Thank you for what? she said to herself as she walked out onto the street. *Thank you for getting my hopes up? For taking just two seconds to look at my work and then dismissing it? For sticking it somewhere where no one can find it?*

Lillian's mood was dark as she returned to the house on Confederate Avenue where she was staying. *What am I supposed to do now?* she wondered. Thankfully her hostess was out making calls. Lillian ran up to her room, closed the door firmly behind her, and threw herself onto the bed. She sobbed until her eyes throbbed and she had drenched three handkerchiefs. Then, exhausted, she drifted off to sleep.

When Lillian awoke, shafts of afternoon sun were streaming through the window. And something felt very different inside her. She remembered that she had been rejected for the job at the newspaper, but it was not a painful recollection. In fact, she felt happy and peaceful and sure of one thing: God knew she would be turned down for the job because He had something better for her to do. Lillian rolled over and reached for her handbag. Inside was Mattie Perry's address. Without a shadow of doubt or regret, Lillian knew that God was leading her to work in the orphanage in North Carolina.

It was three days before Lillian thought about going back to the *Georgian* office to pick up her sketches. When she walked into the newsroom with its bustling energy, she held her head high, confident she was supposed to go to the orphanage.

Mr. Howard sat behind his desk scribbling furiously on a pad. When he looked up and saw Lillian, he beckoned her to his office. He did not look pleased to see her.

"Why didn't you come back, young lady?" he asked sharply. "I held the job open for you for as long as I could, but I had no way to contact you, and so I had to hire someone else yesterday."

Lillian sank into the chair. "But I did come back," she replied. "I came back when you were sick. I spoke to Mr. Whiting, and he told me you'd already found someone who was perfect for the job."

"That was you!" Mr. Howard groaned. "I thought I made it clear to Whiting that if you came back the job was yours." He shook his head. "I can't imagine how he got that mixed up. Look, I even put your sketches in my top drawer with a letter of welcome attached." He slid the drawer open, and sure enough, there were Lillian's sketches and a letter. "I am so sorry," he went on, as he handed Lillian the sketches, "sorry for myself and sorry for you."

Lillian felt like an outsider watching the scene. Once it would have haunted her to think how closely she had been to getting her dream job, but now she was grateful she had not gotten it.

"Don't be sorry for me, Mr. Howard," she said as she stood up to leave. "I have a wonderful life ahead of me. Thank you for everything."

Lillian turned to smile at Mr. Howard. He looked stunned.

Eight days later Lillian was in Marion, North Carolina, knocking at the door of the Faith Orphanage. She had not gone home before heading there, mainly because she knew her parents would not agree with her plan and would probably do all they could to talk her out of it. But deep inside Lillian knew that she was setting out to find her destiny. The feeling that she had described to Anna Mason of something being just out of her reach had evaporated, and she felt confident that God would unfold her future to her.

A week later Lillian needed to remind herself of that conviction. Looking after one hundred children was far more work than she had ever imagined. Her life was a whirl of mending, cooking, and holding crying babies. She went to bed bone tired every night and awoke at the crack of dawn to prepare breakfast. "Living by faith," as Mattie Perry called it, was not easy either. Up until then Lillian's parents had provided all of her needs, but now she had no means of support. When her shoes wore out, she had no money to replace them. She prayed about what to do, and the following day someone donated a box of old clothes that included a pair of half-worn men's shoes. Lillian picked them out of the box and tried them on. They were a little stiff, but they fit, and so she asked Mattie if she could have them.

"But they are men's shoes!" Mattie exclaimed. "My dear, of course you may have them, but do you *want* them? I can't see you wearing something like that."

"Well, I prayed for shoes, and this is what showed up," Lillian said. "I will take them as God's provision for me."

"All right then," Mattie replied.

Lillian was happy with her shoes, though even the children noticed they were out of keeping with the rest of her clothes. She found a sketch one orphan boy had drawn that showed her in an elegant dress with oversized men's shoes sticking out the bottom. Lillian laughed when she saw it. She must look a sight, but she did not care. She was sure she was where God wanted her to be, so what did it matter how she looked?

Over the winter Lillian grew attached to many of the children. She was constantly learning more about each child's personality and the unique way that he or she had been created by God.

Sometimes someone at church or in town would give Lillian a few cents or even a dollar for her own needs, but more often than not, Lillian would hand the money over to Mattie to help pay a bill. There was always enough money to pay for the necessities but never much over.

In the spring Mattie's brother Jason and his wife, Emma, came to visit the orphanage. They were passing through on a preaching trip and stopped to help out. Lillian liked them right away, and they often took her with them on short preaching trips. Lillian soon found that she loved to share the gospel, so when Mattie encouraged her to attend a local Bible college, she did.

For the next five years, Lillian's life was full. She spent part of her time caring for the orphans and part with the Perrys, preaching around the South. On one of these trips, they visited a nearby farming community and stayed with the Goodson family. Jason and Emma knew the family well, and Lillian felt right at home there too, especially around Tom, the oldest son in the family. Tom was tall and muscular, and he was an ordained minister. Lillian was drawn to him right away, and the more time they spent together, the more they liked each other.

A short time later the local schoolhouse hosted a picnic dinner auction to raise money. Lillian prepared a dinner box to be auctioned, and Tom made the highest bid for it. When he walked over to claim the dinner box, he grinned at Lillian. "I hope one day you will be making me dinner every night," he said to her.

A thrill went down Lillian's spine. How glad she was that she had missed out on the job in

Atlanta and had come to the orphanage. Meeting a godly and handsome young man like Tom was more than she could have dreamed of, and she was sure it must be part of God's plan for her life.

By the end of spring, Lillian and Tom were spending all their spare time together, and in May, Tom asked Lillian to marry him. Although Lillian was certain it was the next step for her, she and Tom prayed together about it until they were sure it was the right thing to do. The wedding date was set for two months away, in summer 1910.

Lillian still did not have much money, but thankfully she'd had lots of practice sewing since arriving at the orphanage. Tom's mother bought her a length of white silk, and Lillian set to work sewing her wedding dress.

Everything was right on target, so much so that ten days before the wedding, Lillian had time to accompany Mattie to hear a missionary from India speak. As he spoke, Lillian realized that tears were streaming down her face. She wiped them away, but they continued to flow. Lillian had no idea why this was happening. *Everything in my life is going along so perfectly. Why am I crying?* she asked herself.

When the service was over, it took all of Lillian's energy to greet her neighbors, and for some reason she could not look the missionary in the eye.

When she returned to the orphanage, Lillian asked to be excused and went to her room. Once again she lay on her bed, her body racked with sobs. *If everything is so right, why do things now feel so wrong?* she questioned.

Lillian did not sleep that night. As she pondered the question, she realized she knew the answer. Somewhere deep in her heart, Lillian knew that God had called her to be a missionary—and she felt the call was to go to Africa. Goose bumps covered her arms as she admitted this to herself. But in coming to this realization, she had to face another fact as well: Tom did not have a call to be a missionary.

Just as day was breaking, there was a knock on the door and Mattie popped her head into the room.

"Lillian, if you want to talk about anything, I'm here. Or would you rather I let you alone for the day?"

Lillian sat up and rubbed her eyes. "No, come in," she said. "Sit down."

"You were very upset last night. Would you like to tell me what was wrong?" Mattie asked.

Lillian took a deep breath. She knew she was about to say something that would drastically change the course of her life.

Chapter 4

A Real, Live Missionary

"Nothing is wrong," Lillian said, meeting Mattie's gaze, "except that I know what the next step is for me. I am engaged to the most wonderful man in the world, and I can't marry him."

Mattie drew back. "What do you mean you can't marry him? Everything is arranged, isn't it? You're not short of anything, are you?"

"No, it's not that. Everyone has been so kind. We have everything we need."

"What's the problem then?" Mattie asked in a perplexed voice. "You two are so right for each other. It's wonderful to see you together."

"But that's just it," Lillian said, her tears flowing again. "We can't be together. I am supposed to go to Africa, and Tom feels called to stay here."

39

"You...what?" Mattie blurted.

"It's true," Lillian sobbed. "God has called me to be a missionary, and I can't refuse Him, not even... not even for Tom."

"Oh, poor Tom. How is he ever going to get over this?" Mattie gasped. "I've never seen a young man so in love."

"I know," Lillian said quietly. Then her body shook with sobs. Mattie held Lillian's hand while she calmed down a little.

"I have to tell Tom right away. It isn't fair for him to think we will be married in a week and a half."

Mattie agreed, and two hours later Lillian found herself facing the most difficult task of her young life. Tom was stunned when he heard what she had to say. In fact, he had trouble taking it in. He told Lillian that if she wanted to be a missionary for a year or two, he would wait for her. But Lillian shook her head. Somewhere deep inside she knew for certain that she was called to some foreign place and that she would never live in the United States again.

Eventually she managed to convey this to Tom, and then she returned to the orphanage. As much as she loved the work there, she knew that her time at the orphanage was over as well. She had to get some missionary training. But how? She had only five dollars to her name. She had used the rest of her money to help the orphanage and to pay for wedding preparations.

A week later Lillian heard about a holiness missionary conference to be held in Pittsburgh,

Pennsylvania, and she felt sure that attending it was the first step toward missionary service. But Pittsburgh was over six hundred miles away. As she prayed about attending the conference, several of Lillian's friends gave her money to make the trip.

Within days Lillian had the eighteen dollars needed for the train fare, and she put the money on Mattie's desk so that it could be kept safe. However, before Lillian could tell Mattie that she had put the money there, Mattie's sister Myrtle found it. Assuming it to be orphanage money, she used it to pay the food bill. When the mistake was discovered, there was not enough spare cash at the orphanage to pay back that much money. Lillian was shocked. She was sure that God had provided the money for her to get to the conference, and now the money was gone. She wondered whether perhaps she had not heard God after all.

The more Lillian thought and prayed about it, the more convinced she was that God wanted her to attend the conference. Her friends rallied once again and gave her what spare cash they had. But this time it added up to only ten dollars, enough to take the train only as far as Washington, D.C.

By now Lillian was convinced that she should go as far as she could and trust God to provide the missing money, so she bought a train ticket to Washington. She had never been there before and did not know a single person in the city. Mattie gave her the name of one of her friends in Washington and a letter of introduction. She also promised that as soon as the orphanage had eighteen dollars, she would send it on to Lillian so that she could complete her journey.

As Lillian sat on the train headed north, she tried not to think too much about what she was doing. She had one small bag with her, a dollar in her purse, and the burning desire to be a missionary. Lillian's church in Asheville, the Buxton Street Holiness Church, could not support her financially, and her parents were set against the idea of her new career.

When the train pulled into the station in Washington, D.C., Lillian collected her bag and walked to the house where Mattie's friend, Miss Olivier, lived. She nervously rang the doorbell and straightened her hair. A middle-aged woman opened the door. Lillian explained who she was and handed her Mattie's letter.

"What a shame you have come right now," Miss Olivier said, shaking her head. "Normally I would love to take you in, but right now I have a missionary family and another single missionary from Egypt staying in my spare rooms." She smiled and reached for Lillian's bag. "Still, I am sure you must be hungry. Come in and have lunch with us, and then we'll work out where you can go next."

Lillian said a silent prayer of thanks as she was led into the living room. Perhaps God was working this out after all. If she had gone straight to Pittsburgh, she would not have this opportunity to meet a real, live missionary from Egypt on the northern edge of Africa. Surely he could answer her many questions.

A tall man stood up as Lillian entered the room.

"This is the Reverend Brelsford," Miss Olivier said, "and his wife. And this is Miss Lillian Trasher. She wants to be a missionary to Africa."

"Africa?" Mr. Brelsford echoed. "Sit down, miss, and tell me all about it. What part of Africa are you called to?"

"I don't know," Lillian replied, eager to be the one asking the questions, not answering them. There were so many things she wanted to know.

"Surely your board has some region in mind," the reverend continued.

"Not really," Lillian said, accepting a cup of steaming tea from Miss Olivier. "I'm not being sent out by a board. In fact, I'm not even an official member of a church. I've been attending a holiness church in Asheville, and of course they will be praying for me, but that's about all."

"Well, your family then? I assume they are financing this venture of yours."

Lillian began to feel very awkward. "No, sir," she said. "In fact, they wish I wouldn't go at all."

Mrs. Brelsford spoke for the first time. "You mean you are off to Africa with no support, no idea of where you are going, and only the fare to get there?"

At this Lillian wished she could be almost anywhere else but where she was. Saying her dream out loud made it sound foolish. Still, she decided to be honest.

"Reverend Brelsford," she said, looking him in the eyes, "I have one dollar."

The room was suddenly silent. Mrs. Brelsford sat wide-eyed, her cup of tea halfway to her lips. Mr. Brelsford shook his head. Finally he spoke. "No! No! No! You are off on a fool's errand. There is no place for a girl like you in Africa. You don't know the language. You haven't any support or way of getting it. No! It must not be allowed. You had better go straight home to your parents and tell them you are sorry for ever worrying them with such nonsense."

The rest of the conversation was stilted until another missionary, Mattie Rast, came into the room. Everyone seemed relieved to have someone and something different to focus on. When Mattie heard that Lillian had nowhere to stay, she offered to move out of the room she was staying in and stay with a friend in Washington, D.C. Lillian was very grateful to have somewhere to stay, even though she carefully avoided speaking again about her missionary call.

On the second day of her stay, Lillian was walking down the hallway when the Reverend Brelsford called her into the living room. He cleared his throat. "Miss Trasher, I have something I need to say to you. Please sit down."

Lillian obligingly sat down and waited for the next lecture about going home.

"On discussing things with my wife, and after praying about it, I must confess I was hasty in what

I said yesterday. Can you forgive me for doubting your call?"

Lillian did not reply. She was busy trying to comprehend what she was hearing.

The reverend went on. "It's just that it was so shocking to think that a young girl such as you would dare to venture out to the other side of the world without her family or money or any other arrangements. We are used to doing things in an orderly manner, and it just seemed preposterous to us. However, God does work in mysterious ways, and we can see that you have faith—that is the key. Would you forgive me?"

Lillian smiled. "There isn't anything to forgive," she said. "I understand how foolish it sounds. Sometimes I wonder myself what I am doing. I can't see into the future, but I know that God has called me to be a missionary, and He will open the way for me."

"That's just what I wanted to talk to you about," the reverend went on. "As you know, my wife and I run a mission home in Assiout, Egypt. I am not in a position to offer you money of any kind, but if you find your way to Assiout, we could provide your meals and lodging and you could work with us."

Lillian stood up and walked over to the window. Was it possible that this was God's next step for her? Egypt was a part of the continent of Africa, and it was strange how she had ended up staying in Washington with these missionaries.

As she watched the rain pour down, Lillian's heart flipped with joy. It was the next step for her; she knew it. She turned to Mr. Brelsford, tears streaming down her face. "Thank you. I believe I will take you up on the offer."

That night Lillian could hardly sleep. She had known for several weeks that she was going to be a missionary, but now she knew where—Assiout, Egypt! She studied Miss Olivier's map and found Assiout, located about two hundred miles south of Cairo on the Nile River.

The next day the eighteen dollars arrived from Mattie Perry, and Lillian was able to take the train the rest of the way to Pittsburgh.

The conference was even more wonderful than Lillian had imagined it would be. By the end of it, Lillian was convinced that God had called her to Egypt. She did not, however, have enough money to travel farther than New York City. Undeterred, she set off to the train station with Mr. Brelsford, who had also attended the conference. The reverend was heading south on a mission tour before returning to Egypt. When he came to buy his ticket, he discovered that he was several dollars short of the fare. Without thinking about her own needs, Lillian pulled out her purse and gave him the shortfall in the ticket price. It was only after she had waved goodbye to the reverend that Lillian counted her money. She now had only enough money to make it as far as Harrisburg, Pennsylvania.

As Lillian boarded the train, she recalled that a friend in the church in Asheville had sent her the address of a Christian couple in Harrisburg. Once again Lillian found an unknown house, introduced herself, and was given a meal and a bed for the night.

As she prayed that night, Lillian felt that she would be in New York by Sunday. The following morning she asked to stay two more days, until Saturday morning. Then the husband offered to escort her to the train station. Lillian said nothing about her lack of money, and as the two of them approached the ticket office, the man said, "Do you have the money for your fare ready?"

"No," Lillian replied. "I don't have the money ready for my fare. In fact, I don't have any money at all."

The man turned and stared at her. Then he shook his head. "Of course, I will be glad to pay for you to get to New York, but that is nothing compared to the amount you will need to get to Egypt. How do you expect to get there?"

Lillian smiled. "If God wants me there, God will get me there. I believe He is looking after that need right now."

"I see," the man replied, taking his wallet from his pocket. "I hope you are right."

Lillian thanked him and once again boarded the train. She arrived in New York City hot and exhausted but glad that the first stage of her journey was over. It was July 1910, and she made her way to the Glad Tidings Mission, where she stayed for a time.

Lillian spoke at the mission on Sunday. Soon she was invited to speak at various mission meetings and churches around the city. A collection was often taken for her, and by the end of August, she had saved forty dollars. She took all of her money to the Thomas Cook Travel office and put down a deposit on a passage to Egypt. She still needed sixty dollars, but she was confident that the rest of the money would come in. She wrote to her parents and her sister Jennie, telling them that she was sailing for the African continent on October 8.

Lillian's parents did not reply right away, but Jennie did, with a most startling proposal. Jennie wrote that she was worried that Lillian would get sick on the voyage and have no one to care for her, so she was going to come along too. This was financially possible because Jennie had bought a rental cottage beside her own cottage in Long Beach, and if she rented them both, she would have enough money to live on for a few months. Jennie added that she intended to stay in Egypt only long enough to see that Lillian was properly settled. Lillian was delighted with this news. How wonderful it would be to have her sister along for the journey.

October 6—the day before Jennie was due to get to New York—finally arrived. Lillian still owed the remaining sixty dollars on her ticket, a fact she dreaded sharing with Jennie, who did not understand Lillian's faith in God. That day Lillian lay on her bed feeling sick with anxiety. She was the only one in the Glad Tidings Mission at that time of day, and so when she heard a loud knock at the door, she felt obliged to get up and see who it was. Lillian stumbled to the door, where a stranger stood.

"May I come in?" the woman asked.

"Certainly," Lillian replied, holding the door wide.

"Good," the woman said, bustling past her. "You must be Lillian Trasher. I have to ask, what are your plans."

Lillian felt too sick to say much, and she had no idea who this woman was. She answered the question briefly, telling the woman that she was on her way to Assiout, Egypt, on October 8.

The woman kept probing her with questions: What did Lillian want to do in Egypt? Who was going with her? How much money did it cost to get there?

Lillian answered each question in a daze and then watched in astonishment as the woman knelt in front of her and began to pray, thanking God for providing for all Lillian's needs. Lillian closed her eyes as the woman prayed.

Then, as suddenly as she had got down on her knees, the woman jumped up. "I must go," she said as she unclipped her purse. She reached in and then handed something to Lillian. "Here, take this."

Without another word the woman left. Lillian unfolded her hand. In it was sixty dollars! She had her fare to Egypt after all. She rushed to the door to see which direction the woman had headed, but the woman had already melted into the crowd in the street.

"Thank You, Jesus, thank You!" Lillian exclaimed as she sat down on a nearby chair.

The following day Lillian met Jennie at the train station and told her the ticket was paid for. Jennie went straight to the Thomas Cook office herself and paid for the ticket Lillian had booked for her.

That night the two sisters went to a missionary meeting. Fifty dollars was collected for Lillian at the meeting, and someone pressed another twenty dollars in her hand as she left. Lillian was thrilled. She wrote in her diary that night, "My God shall supply all your needs." *And surely it has been so thus far*, she thought. She had left North Carolina with one dollar in her pocket, and now, three months later, she was on the eve of embarking for Egypt.

Early the next morning Lillian was excited to finally board the SS *Berlin*. Several of her friends from the Glad Tidings Mission came on board to say a final goodbye. One of them said, "Lillian, before we go, why don't you open your Bible and read the first verse you see."

Lillian took up the challenge. She closed her eyes and flicked through the pages. She stopped, pointed her finger at the page, and read the verse under it. "I have surely seen the affliction of my people which are in Egypt, and have heard their groanings…and I am come down to deliver them.… and now come, I will send thee into Egypt."

"That is amazing," her friend exclaimed. "I have never heard that verse before."

"Neither have I," Lillian replied, noting the goose bumps on her arms. "I wonder what lies ahead for me."

Chapter 5

Assiout

On November 10, 1910, one month and two days after setting sail from New York, Lillian caught her first glance of Alexandria, Egypt. It was dawn, and she had asked the steward to wake her as soon as the coast came into view. Now she stood on deck, watching long stretches of white sand beach lapped by the blue water of the Mediterranean Sea. At the far end of the beach, the outline of the ancient port city peeked above the horizon. The city's whitewashed buildings gleamed in the early morning sun.

Most of the passengers on board the SS *Berlin* were excited about the prospect of docking in Alexandria and then seeing the Pyramids and the Sphinx at Giza, but Lillian had much more important things to occupy her mind. Somewhere out there, three hundred miles south of Alexandria, lay the city of Assiout, and that was where her heart was.

As the morning sun continued to rise ahead of them, other passengers, including Jennie, joined Lillian on deck and watched in awe as the ship made its way into Alexandria's harbor. The sight was unlike anything Lillian had seen before. The buildings rose up from the harbor's edge. Their weathered mud-brick facades gave them an ancient air, and laden camels and donkeys pulling carts wove in and out between them. As the ship approached the dock, a noisy, teeming crowd of people awaited the vessel's arrival.

Lillian was so enthralled by the scene before her that she hardly noticed that the ship had tied up alongside the dock and passengers were beginning to disembark. Quickly she ran below deck to her cabin and threw the last few items into her trunk. It was time to go!

"Miss Trasher, Miss Trasher!" Lillian heard the voice calling her among the crowd of people that swirled around the bottom of the gangplank. She waved, glad that she was tall enough to see over just about everyone's head. A young man waved back and maneuvered his way through the throng to get to Lillian.

"I am Kamil. Mr. Brelsford sent me from Assiout. You are the one, right?" He spoke with a proper English accent that made Lillian want to laugh.

"Yes," she replied. "And this is my sister, Jennie Trasher. It is so exciting to be here! If you could help us get our trunks and go through customs and immigration, we will be our way."

"Indeed," Kamil replied. "I know exactly how to get through all of this. Follow me."

True to his word, in less than an hour, Kamil safely guided the two women through the official formalities for landing in Egypt. Soon the three of them were on their way across the city in a horse-drawn carriage. Lillian sat fascinated as they rolled past busy bazaars filled with merchants selling brightly colored fruits and vegetables, water in goatskin bags, brassware, bolts of cloth, and all manner of other items. Everywhere people swarmed around. They overflowed from narrow alleys that passed for streets onto the avenue that the threesome was riding along. The air was damp and pungent, and the midmorning sun beat down baking the whole scene.

Finally the trio arrived at a train station. Kamil arranged for the trunks to be loaded into the baggage car and then helped Lillian and Jennie into the third-class carriage. He explained that their next stop would be Cairo, 110 miles to the southeast, and then it was on to Assiout. Just as she had on the carriage ride, Lillian strained to take in every detail: the mud huts that lined the Nile River, the men guiding donkeys carrying backbreaking loads, the date palms that seemed to grow everywhere, and the waterwheels pumping water from the Nile into the labyrinth of irrigation canals that fanned out into the parched countryside. Lillian was struck by how timeless everything looked. Apart from the railway tracks, she could see no signs of "modern civilization." Lillian felt like she was looking at a scene right out of a Bible story.

The train stopped in Cairo, and Kamil advised the women to stay seated. Lillian sat watching as men and women balancing baskets on their heads claimed seats on the train for the journey south. She watched as some of the boys threw their baskets through the open windows of the carriage onto seats they wanted and then dived through the window after them. As in Alexandria, the station platform in Cairo teemed with people. Lillian noticed a blind man squatting on the far side of the platform begging for money. It was all so very different from New York or Asheville or Atlanta.

Soon the train lurched, and they were off again on the final two hundred miles of their journey. As they left Cairo behind, the sky began to turn a golden color. Kamil told Lillian that the color was the result of sand swirling in the wind. Lillian thought it beautiful. The gold cast gave everything such a rich glow as the train made its way deeper into the broad Nile River valley.

"Assiout," Kamil finally announced proudly, "the most beautiful city in Egypt."

Lillian gasped. She had come to Egypt thinking she would be living in a desert. No one had told her how beautiful Assiout was. The city was set beside the Nile. The land around the city was particularly lush and green, and it was as if the palm trees that grew everywhere wrapped the place in a green blanket. A hill rose behind the city, and Kamil pointed out that it was known as the Hill of the Hermits.

When the train hissed to a stop in Assiout, Kamil guided Lillian and Jennie from the carriage and made sure that their trunks were unloaded onto the station platform. Then he hired a horse and cart—not nearly as fancy as the one in Alexandria—and everyone climbed aboard. Lillian tried to memorize every street corner and every building as they rolled along, hoping that these streets would soon be as familiar to her as the ones back home in North Carolina.

Within minutes the cart pulled to a halt outside a long, low building.

"We are here," Kamil announced, "and ahead of time too."

Lillian jumped down from the cart and adjusted her hat. She knew she must look quite a sight after so many hours of traveling in a hot, dusty train. But she did not care; she had arrived! Lillian was finally standing outside the mission house in Assiout, Egypt. Goose bumps covered her arms as she walked up the brick path toward the door.

Before she reached the door, it burst open and Mrs. Brelsford came scurrying out. "Welcome, welcome!" she said. "Come in and have a cup of tea. You must be exhausted."

It did not take long for Lillian to feel quite at home in the mission house. The house was the hub of activity for the holiness missionaries in the area. Lillian felt instantly drawn to one of the missionaries,

Sela Friend, an older woman with an air of confidence about her. Sela, more than anyone else, helped to ease Lillian into mission life. She spent hours teaching Lillian basic Arabic and showing her around the ancient sections of the city. On these rambling adventures, Sela often told Lillian about the history of Assiout. She explained that the city had been home to Coptic Christians for centuries. The Coptic Church in Egypt originated near Alexandria, where, over nineteen hundred years before, St. Mark had founded the first Christian church in Egypt. Many people had accepted the gospel message, and now many of their descendants lived in and around Assiout.

Jennie sometimes came along as Sela and Lillian traipsed around the city but not often. After all, she was there not to be a missionary but merely to see that her sister was safe and happy. When she was assured of that, she would be returning to her life in California.

After Lillian had been in Assiout three weeks, Sela began taking her to visit the local women. Lillian was amazed at how polite and hospitable these women were. At one house they visited, the family killed and cooked their last chicken so that Sela and Lillian could eat with them. Lillian was deeply touched by the gesture.

Before they knew it, winter was upon them. The nights grew cold, and Lillian and Jennie huddled together for warmth. Lillian's last prayer before dropping off to sleep at night was often for the poor families in the city who could not afford blankets to keep them warm.

Lillian knew that Jennie did not like cold weather, but every time she asked her sister when she was returning to the United States, Jennie would say that she wanted to stay a little longer.

Everything went smoothly until late one Sunday afternoon in February 1911, about three months after Lillian's arrival in Assiout. Lillian could not explain what bothered her, but she felt certain something was about to go wrong. She did not share her foreboding with Jennie; it would have been pointless to worry her. Instead Lillian prayed and waited.

That night, after dinner and house prayers, Lillian heard a loud banging at the door. She jumped up to open the door and was confronted by a man with a desperate look on his face. Even with her limited Arabic, Lillian could tell that the man wanted someone to come with him quickly.

Kamil came up behind her. "He says a young mother is dying and he wants someone to help her," he translated for Lillian.

Somehow Lillian knew that this man had come for her.

"Let me go, please," she said, turning to the Reverend Brelsford.

The reverend looked around the table, but no one else showed any interest in going out so late at night. "Very well," he said. "Take Kamil with you as an escort."

"I'll come with you if you like," Sela offered.

"Please do," Lillian replied, suddenly thinking of the situation she could be about to step into. Sela reached for her blue, woolen cape.

"Be careful, Lillian," Jennie whispered as she handed Lillian a scarf. From her comment, Lillian wondered whether Jennie also had been feeling that something significant was going to happen.

Soon the three mission workers were hurrying down the dark streets. Within minutes they came to an area of town that Lillian was not familiar with. It was down by the Nile River, and the houses were nothing more than squat mud huts with low doors and no windows. In the moonlight the trio's guide led them through a maze of these huts, until he ducked into one. Lillian and the others followed and found themselves in pitch darkness. Lillian left the door to the hut ajar behind her and waited while her eyes adjusted to the blackness. In the dim moonlight that spilled in through the open door, she made out an old woman sitting with a bundle in her lap as well as the silhouette of a girl lying against the far wall. Lillian knelt down beside the girl and felt her pulse. It was faint. The girl stirred, opened her eyes, and then grabbed Lillian's arm with a surprisingly strong grip.

"*Arjouky, arjouky,*" she pleaded.

Lillian knew that the Arabic word *arjouky* meant "please" in English.

"Ask her what she wants," Lillian said, turning to Kamil.

No sooner had she said this than a thin wail rose from the bundle on the old woman's lap. It was the unmistakable cry of a baby. Lillian scrambled to her feet and held out her hands to take the baby. She walked to the doorway to examine the child in the moonlight. Lillian shrank back in horror at the sight of the baby, which looked like a skeleton with a paper bag stretched over it. The child stank, and two large, unblinking eyes were the only things that reminded Lillian that it was human.

The baby began to wail again, and as Lillian continued to look at it, a wave of love flowed over her. This frail child was starving to death, and its mother, a girl of no more than fifteen or sixteen, was probably dying. The old woman, a great grandmother, Lillian supposed, sat motionless, staring at the scene. Tears began to trickle down Lillian's cheeks as she thought of the hopelessness that engulfed the family and the short future this child had. Taking a deep breath, Lillian leaned over and kissed the baby. Then she looked over at the mother.

"*Arjouky, takhdihom,*" the girl said and then fell silent.

Sela bent down and felt for a pulse. "She's dead," she said quietly. "God be with her."

Kamil turned to Lillian. "Do you know what the mother said before she died?"

Lillian shook her head. "I know *arjouky* means 'please,' but I didn't recognize the other word."

"*Takhdihom* means 'take her.' Mees Lillian, the mother wanted you to take the baby."

Lillian stood rooted to the spot. Other than the whimpering of the baby, no sound was heard. The young man who had guided them to the mud house slipped out into the night and was gone before anyone could ask him a question.

Finally Kamil broke the silence. "Of course, you cannot think of keeping the baby," he said. "The old woman will find a way to deal with it. It won't live long anyway."

Now that conversation had started again, the old woman stood up. She barely came up to Lillian's waist. *"Menfedlock takode el baby,"* she said, then her voice rose higher. *"Arma marifish irmel a beha!"*

Kamil shrugged his shoulders and turned to Lillian. "She says she also wants you to take the baby. She doesn't know what to do with it."

Lillian watched as the woman stepped out the door and gestured toward the river. She mumbled something under her breath.

"What did she say?" Lillian whispered to Kamil.

"She said, 'It's only a girl anyway. What does it matter if she dies.'"

Indignation rose in Lillian. Was the old woman thinking of drowning the baby if they left her behind? Lillian was holding a human being, a scrap of a human being clinging to life but a human being nonetheless.

Without stopping to think about what she was doing, Lillian held the baby close to her heart as she brushed past Sela and Kamil. With long strides she set out for the mission station alone. "I will find a way to care for you," she whispered to the baby as she hurried along the path. "Surely the Reverend and Mrs. Brelsford will let me take in a desperate little one like you."

Chapter 6

Fareida

The way was unfamiliar, and Lillian stumbled over rocks and bushes as she carried the baby back to the mission house. She walked much slower than Kamil and Sela, and it was a full hour before Lillian slipped through the back door of the mission and tiptoed to the room she shared with Jennie.

"Kamil and Sela are back already, and they told me you had the baby," Jennie said, standing up to greet her sister. "Let's take a look."

Lillian walked over and showed Jennie the baby.

"We have to get those clothes off her and bathe her. The poor little thing," Lillian said as she eyed the baby's filthy clothes in full light for the first time. "Look, they have sewed her into them. No wonder she smells so bad. There's no way to change her diaper."

Jennie moved toward the door. "I already have some milk. I'll warm it on the kerosene heater while you undress her. I also got a pile of clean rags from the cleaning cupboard. They should make good diapers for now."

Lillian spread one of the rags on her bedspread and laid the baby down. Then, very carefully, she began to cut the gown off the baby. As she worked, she hummed the chorus of a hymn. She was determined that the child would not see her recoil with disgust as she wiped her bottom. When she had removed the garment, she could see that the baby's skin was raw and tender. The baby's little bones reminded Lillian of a chicken.

Sela knocked quietly and entered the room. She smiled at Lillian, then gathered up an old sheet and cut from it the pattern of a simple baby gown. She sat down beside the mantle lamp and started to sew the pieces of the gown together. Lillian gave her a grateful look just as Jennie returned with some warm milk and a bucket of warm water.

Lillian held the baby over the bucket and gently sponged her body. The child let out a loud wail, the volume of which surprised Lillian.

"Hush, hush," she crooned. "You will have milk in a moment."

The bath took some time, and Lillian was not altogether pleased with the results. Although the baby's hair was now unmatted and the filth was gone from her body, she still smelled terrible. Lillian decided that the smell was rotting flesh, and she determined to keep the wounds clean and give the baby plenty of fresh air and sunshine.

Soon Lillian was feeding her new charge one eyedropper of milk at a time. She remembered all the little orphans she had fed at the orphanage in North Carolina, and she was grateful for the experience, though none of the children there had been as starved as this frail baby was.

Even with her child-care experience, Lillian was unable to coax much milk into the baby's mouth and even less down her throat. The baby cried for most of the night, stopping only when she was so exhausted that she fell asleep for a few minutes. At every opportunity Lillian dropped milk into her tiny mouth and massaged her throat so that she would swallow it.

Lillian was concerned that the crying would keep the other missionaries in the house awake, as the walls were paper thin. But there was nothing she could do about it. She was already doing all she knew how to do to calm the child. Jennie hardly slept that night either.

By breakfast time the women had decided on an Arabic name for the baby—Fareida. Lillian and Jennie spent the entire day caring for Fareida. They took turns attempting to feed her and sewing clothes for her. That night the baby again cried constantly, and the following morning she looked thinner than ever. Lillian thought that Fareida was dying, but she would not give up.

For the next ten days Lillian's and Jennie's lives revolved around the baby. Every mouthful of milk swallowed was a victory and every minute of sleep a relief. As the days rolled by, Lillian noticed that the other missionaries in the house were becoming more stressed out. They had bags under their eyes and yawned at the breakfast table. Several of them remarked about how little the baby slept and how strong her lungs were.

Finally, after Fareida had clung to life for two weeks, the Reverend Brelsford asked Lillian one morning to come to his office. Lillian left Jennie with Fareida and proceeded with a sense of dread.

Mr. Brelsford invited Lillian to sit down and then got straight to the point. "We have had a meeting, and we all agree that this mission house is no place for a very sick baby. She cries all night and keeps us awake, and then we don't have the energy to go on with our regular missionary activities during the day." He paused to look at Lillian and then continued. "I am sorry, but you will have to take her back."

Lillian gasped. "Back? Back where? She has no place to go. Her mother is dead, and I don't know who the old woman and the man were. I can't take her back."

"You have to," Mr. Brelsford said, "at once. She cannot spend another night in this house."

"But back where?" Lillian repeated. She knew she sounded stupid, but she could hardly grasp that the mission leader would want her to abandon the baby. "Is there an orphanage she could go to?" Lillian finally asked.

Mr. Brelsford shook his head. "There is no such thing as an orphanage in Egypt. Just think how many children would be clamoring to get in if there were one. No, you will have to find some relative to take the baby."

Lillian shuddered as she thought of the old woman who had been holding Fareida when the baby's mother died and of her staring into the Nile. Surely the baby would end up there if she were returned to her. Lillian felt her eyes blurring with tears. She wanted to ask this missionary how he could turn a needy child away, but she held her tongue. It was no use challenging Mr. Brelsford's authority in the mission house. Instead Lillian stood and walked to the door. Before she left the room, she turned and said, "All right. You are asking me to take her back. I will take her back, and I will go with her." She watched as a frown spread over the reverend's face.

"Alone?" Mr. Brelsford spluttered. "Lillian, if you had been here longer, you would realize that this is quite impossible. A lone American woman living in an Arabic world. You will be killed, or you'll starve to death."

By now Lillian's own words had begun to give her courage, and she knew she was doing the right thing. "I won't be alone. I will have God with me," she retorted.

"Umm...I..." Mr. Brelsford seemed lost for words. Finally he stood up and looked Lillian in the eye. "Very well, don't say I didn't warn you. If you leave this house with the baby, you leave without my permission. Go and do what you want, but if things go wrong, don't come back here begging for help."

Lillian stood rooted to the spot for a moment. She could scarcely reconcile the harshness of the Reverend Brelsford's speech with the man she had met in Washington, D.C., the previous fall. Then she stumbled out the door.

Lillian needed fresh air. She left the house and began walking down the dusty road. *What have I done?* she asked herself. As if to answer the question, her mind reflected on the nativity story of Mary and Joseph searching for a room in Bethlehem. There was no room at the inn for the baby Jesus to be born in, and it appeared that there was no room in the mission house for another baby who needed shelter. Lillian tried not to dwell on the unfairness of it all. Instead she tried to think of a place where an American woman and a sick baby could stay.

As she walked, Lillian recalled a narrow, three-story house she had seen for rent on one of her visits around the city with Sela. She wondered if the place was still available. Although she was unsure of exactly where she had seen it, Lillian had a general idea. She headed in that direction, praying that the house would come into view.

Sure enough, Lillian found the house and with relief noted that it was still for rent. She managed to find the owner, who lived next door, and with her limited Arabic conveyed to him that she wanted to rent the house. The owner nodded and told her the house cost two pounds a month. Then he unlocked the door and showed Lillian inside. The house was dirty and full of cobwebs, but underneath Lillian could see that it was strongly built. Some hard scrubbing would restore the tiled floors to a shine. As a bonus, from the third-story window, Lillian caught a glimpse of the Nile River

"I'll take it," Lillian told the owner, reaching into her pocket. For some reason that morning she had felt that she should take all her money out of her suitcase and put it in her skirt pocket. Now she knew why. The owner smiled and accepted the money. The deal was done. Lillian now had a place of her own in which to live. Without wasting any time, she went to the nearby market and bought a table, four chairs, some blankets, and a kerosene stove for cooking. She decided not to "waste" money on a bed; she would make one out of palm branches.

Lillian paid a teenage boy to carry the items back to her house, and it was only as she arranged the new furniture that the most obvious thought struck her. What about Jennie? What would Jennie think about living among the Egyptians? Would she agree with Mr. Brelsford that it was a crazy scheme? Lillian groaned. Right now Jennie was back in their room taking care of Fareida. She probably assumed that Lillian was still talking to Mr. Brelsford, and here was Lillian, standing in a newly rented and furnished house! It was one thing to volunteer herself for this new life, but she should have asked Jennie if she wanted to be part of it. Lillian had no doubt, though, that Jennie would come with her. Although Jennie was nine years older than she was, Lillian had always been the adventurous leader in the family and Jennie the retiring follower. Lillian hated to think that in her impulsiveness she had taken that lead role for granted.

Lillian locked the door of her new house behind her and hurried back to the mission to tell Jennie what she had done. Jennie, who had become just as attached to little Fareida as Lillian, agreed that her younger sister had done the right thing in moving out to protect the baby.

"I have two pounds left," Lillian confided in her sister as the two women packed their few belongings in a trunk. "If we eat local food from the market, we should have enough to eat until the end of the month. After that we will just have to trust God, won't we?"

Jennie nodded in agreement just as Mr. Brelsford arrived at the open door of their room.

"Ah, hum," he said, announcing his arrival.

Lillian felt her heart pound and her hands sweat as she turned to face him. Mr. Brelsford looked grave.

"I have come to ask you to reconsider, Lillian," he said in a fatherly voice. "There is no need for you to leave this place, or Jennie for that matter. You are two single women, and you have security, protection, and food here. What will you have if you leave? Nothing. Who will come to your aid if a man breaks into your house? How will you get food for yourself, much less for this poor baby?" He paused for a moment and then continued. "Take her back to her own people. That's all I am asking. She belongs with them. It's hardly likely that she is going to survive anyway. Why risk everything for a sickly baby?"

Lillian would have been angry at what he was saying except that she knew that he really was worried about her and did want her to be safe. She measured her words carefully. "Please don't worry about us, Mr. Brelsford. We'll be fine. The Lord is with us, and He will not allow any harm to come to us."

Lillian watched as Mr. Brelsford opened his mouth as if to speak and then shut it again. He shook his head as he turned and walked away.

A few minutes later two of the missionary women came into the room. They looked terrified. "Something very bad could happen to you," one of them said.

Lillian did not answer, so the woman turned to Jennie. "Please think of your safety. You could stay even if Lillian goes. There's no need for both of you to be lost. Be sensible," she begged.

Jennie shook her head. "I will go wherever Lillian goes. Remember Ruth and Naomi in the Bible? I suppose I am the Ruth in the story. I have cast my lot with Lillian, and I will not let her go without me."

Lillian wiped a tear from her cheek as she realized once again the complete trust Jennie had in her and her mission. What a huge responsibility it was.

Hearing a whistle at the window, Lillian peered out to see a man with a donkey standing there. Their transportation had arrived. Quietly Lillian picked up the sleeping baby and carried her to the door. Just then Sela walked into the room. Their eyes met, and neither of them needed to say anything. Lillian knew that Sela believed in what she was doing, even before Sela took off her blue, woolen cape and placed it around Lillian's shoulders. The cape enveloped Fareida as well.

"Here, you will both need this," Sela said. "When you put it on, remember that I am praying for you. If you need me, you know where to find me."

The two women embraced for a long time, and then Sela helped Lillian carry her belongings to the waiting donkey.

It was midafternoon when Lillian, Jennie, and the baby set out following the donkey to their new home. Lillian found it strange to think that only five hours earlier she'd had no intention of going anywhere. And now here she was about to move into a new home with Jennie and a baby.

The narrow house was just as Lillian had left it. A small crowd gathered to watch the two American women and the tiny Arab baby move in. Lillian could not blame the people for being curious about them; she knew they were an unusual sight.

That night Lillian wrote the day's date, February 10, 1911, on a slip of paper and placed it in the back of her Bible. Then she opened the well-worn book to Psalm 37 and read, "The steps of a good man are ordered by the LORD: and he delighteth in his way....I have been young, and now am old; yet have I not seen the righteous forsaken, nor his seed begging for bread. He is ever merciful, and lendeth; and his seed is blessed."

"God," Lillian prayed, "we have only You now. I believe You are guiding our steps. You promise that we will not have to beg for bread and that Fareida will become a blessing. Thank You for that promise."

With a quiet excitement about what tomorrow would bring, Lillian Trasher drifted off to sleep on her palm-branch mattress, the blue cape firmly tucked around her and baby Fareida sleeping peacefully beside her.

Chapter 7

Plague

"Look, Jennie, Fareida has grown!" Lillian exclaimed as she dressed the child in a clean baby gown before placing her in a box crib for a morning nap. "Three weeks ago, when we made this gown, it hung on her. Now look. It almost has to stretch to go around her belly."

Jennie walked over to the baby and laughed. "She surely has grown. Oh, Lillian, who would have thought it? She now drinks out of a bottle and sleeps for six hours at a stretch. God has been good to us."

Lillian nodded. "And the neighbors haven't bothered us a bit either. Things are going well."

Even as she spoke these last words, Lillian thought about the empty cupboard in the kitchen. Although she and Jennie had been frugal, their money was all spent, and there was little food left in the house—perhaps enough canned milk to last Fareida another day. And the rent was due.

Once the baby was settled, Lillian climbed the stairs to the third floor of the house, where she liked to pray. She sat down on a chair and put her head in her hands. Suddenly a warm feeling engulfed her, and a thought lodged deep in her heart. *Everything is going to work out. I have been sent to Egypt to found a Christian orphanage.* Lillian sat stunned. An orphanage in Egypt? But it felt so right, as if she had known all along that this was what she was to do.

When Fareida awoke before lunch, Lillian opened the second-to-last can of milk for her to feed on. As she opened the can, her heart soared. "Now I will see God in action," she said to herself.

The following morning, with the excitement of starting an orphanage still burning in her mind, Lillian heard a knock at the door. A messenger boy was delivering a note from Sela inviting Lillian to meet her for dinner later in the week. Lillian thanked the boy, who looked to be about twelve years old, but he did not seem in any hurry to leave.

"Is there something I can help you with?" she asked the boy in Arabic.

"I have a sore head, ma'am," he replied.

Lillian smiled. "I have some medicine that should help you. Would you like an aspirin?"

The boy nodded, and Lillian invited him inside while she rummaged around in her trunk to find the pill bottle.

"Here you are," she said when she found the bottle.

The boy took the pill offered to him and swallowed it, but he still did not look ready to leave. He pointed to Fareida. "Are you the lady looking for children who need a home?" he asked.

Lillian wondered what he was talking about. Then she recalled that the previous afternoon, in her excitement, she had told an Egyptian clerk she was starting an orphanage and how Fareida was her first orphan. The clerk must have spread the word around the neighborhood.

A puzzled look came over the boy's face. "I just want to know," he blurted out, "if you are going to get enough money to look after hundreds of children."

Lillian smiled at his use of the word *hundreds*. She had just one baby at the moment, and that was quite enough to handle. "I know that God is going to provide for all our needs. I don't even know where our next meal is coming from, but I know that God will provide it for us," she told the boy.

The boy's eyes grew wide as he looked from Lillian to the baby. Then he reached into his pocket and pulled out something that he put in Lillian's hand before running out the door.

When Lillian looked down, she saw that he had thrust seven piasters into her hand. Enough money to buy two days' worth of food! Tears filled her eyes as she realized she was holding a miracle. A poor Muslim boy had just given her, a Christian woman, his precious money to help feed a tiny baby. A Bible verse sprang to her mind. "Despise not the day of small beginnings." A contribution of seven piasters was a small beginning, but it opened the door to huge possibilities.

Lillian bought bread, cereal, and milk for the "orphanage" with the money.

Soon word spread about her mission, and small amounts of money or food began to appear on the doorstep. Lillian and Jennie were thrilled that some of their neighbors supported their work, though others did not. Lillian heard rumors that some people believed she was going to gather up orphans and take them back to the United States. Another rumor suggested that she wanted to get the children strong and healthy so that she could sell them as slaves. Lillian tried not to dwell on such matters. She knew that the idea of a foreign woman helping children and babies was unheard of in Assiout, but she had confidence that if she were patient, those around her would come to see her motives.

When they had been living in the house for about two months, a man told Lillian about two small children in a neighboring village. Their parents had died, and an uncle had taken the children in temporarily but was looking for a permanent home for them. Egyptian law forbade anyone other than immediate family adopting an orphan, but the man asked Lillian if she wanted to take them in and raise them as if they were her own.

Lillian's heart skipped a beat. Of course there was room for two more children in the orphanage.

That would bring the number of children she was caring for to three.

That afternoon Lillian hired a donkey and rode out to the village. She had no difficulty locating the children; everyone in the village knew about the two orphans. They turned out to be a girl aged six and a boy aged four. Lillian hugged them and promised that she would look after them and be a mother to them.

As the three of them rode "home," Lillian wondered what the children should call her. She hadn't had to think about this before because Fareida was too young to talk. By the time they entered Assiout, Lillian had made up her mind. "You can call me Mama Lillian," she told the children, who nodded shyly.

The two children fit into the household well, and they loved to entertain Fareida and make her smile.

In July 1911 Lillian heard of another homeless child, and she welcomed him to live in her home. His name was Habib, and he was five years old. The day after his arrival, however, Habib was running such a high fever that Lillian rushed to get a doctor from American Presbyterian Hospital. Soon the doctor was examining Habib. He shook his head when he was finished. "I don't know how to tell you this, but Habib has bubonic plague."

"Bubonic plague!" Lillian repeated incredulously. "One of my children has bubonic plague?"

"I'm afraid so. I will have to take Habib back to the isolation ward at the hospital, and the health inspector will call on you to tell you what to do next. In the meantime, you or anyone else who lives here must not leave the house," the doctor said.

"Very well," Lillian said, bending down to hug Habib goodbye. She was determined to show him love regardless of his condition.

An hour later two health inspectors arrived at the door. They were brief but thorough. They asked for everything in the house that was made of fabric, wood, or metal to be brought into the living room. Then they hauled a large tank from a cart and placed it on the floor, where they filled it with bottles of disinfectant. All the items that had been gathered into the living room were dipped into the liquid, ruining many of them. Next, the inspectors ordered that Fareida and the other two children be kept in isolation for at least ten days. Chances were, they informed Lillian, that the other children would come down with the deadly disease as well.

When the inspectors left the house, Lillian looked around in despair. She wondered how things had gone wrong so quickly. The day before, she and Jennie had been welcoming a new child into their home, and today that child was in isolation in the hospital and almost all of her belongings were saturated. The whole place reeked of disinfectant.

Lillian and Jennie managed to get through the rest of the day. But the following morning, when Lillian examined Fareida and the other two children, she was shocked to discover that they, too, were covered with angry red sores. Lillian fell to her knees.

"Lord," she prayed, "what will I do now? What will I do now?"

In truth, there was only one thing she could do—fetch the doctor again. She and Jennie watched anxiously as he examined the children, but the diagnosis was not what Lillian expected. The children had the measles! This time Lillian sank to her knees with a prayer of thanksgiving. But it was not over yet. That night Lillian could not sleep. The air seemed unusually hot and the room stuffy. Finally, around two in the morning, she found herself gasping for air.

"Jennie," she yelled, "I need you."

Thankfully Jennie was a light sleeper, and within a minute she had a thermometer in Lillian's mouth and was sponging her down with cold water. Jennie drew a deep breath as she read the thermometer under the lamplight.

"One hundred and six degrees. Lillian, you are burning up. I have to get the doctor right away. Here, take a sip of water before I go."

Lillian tried to lift her head, but she did not have the strength to do so. Instead Jennie spooned some water into her sister's mouth. Then she dressed quickly and left the house.

So many things happened quickly after that, but they were a blur to Lillian. She remembered having the doctor feel her pulse and then being propped up and strapped to a chair. Several people, including Sela, carried her in the chair to the hospital. The last thing Lillian remembered before she drifted off into unconsciousness was a muffled conversation between Jennie and the doctor.

Lillian had bubonic plague, and her life hung in the balance for several days. Thankfully, though, after several days she began to grow stronger, as did Habib. Both of them survived their bout with the plague.

Two weeks passed before Lillian was well enough to go home. When she did go home, the doctor ordered her to rest for at least half of each day. He explained that the disease had stressed her heart and she needed to take her recuperation seriously.

For the first two days Lillian tried her best to rest, but it seemed impossible. Habib was now home, too, but he was still listless and required help with feeding. Fareida and the other two children also needed care.

The doctor told Lillian that she needed to come back to the hospital once a week for a checkup. On Thursday, when she set out for her first checkup, Lillian was shocked to find five of her new neighborhood friends standing on her stoop waiting to accompany her. She tried to dissuade them from going along, but they insisted, and so they all set out for the hospital together.

At the hospital the doctor's comments were stern. He told Lillian that she must find a way to rest; her heart needed it. Her friends also insisted on her listening to what the doctor had to say. "You must take a holiday and get your strength back," they urged her.

Lillian felt stubbornness rising within her. She had important things to do. She simply could not afford the time to be an invalid.

"You don't understand, Miss Trasher," the doctor said in a gentle voice. "You will not be able to continue your work unless you rest. Your heart has been severely strained over the past few weeks. I hate to be this blunt, but if you do not take a break, it could stop beating."

Lillian was stunned. It seemed she had no choice. But how could she afford to take a holiday, and who would help Jennie with the children?

Back at the house, one of her neighborhood friends stepped forward and thrust something into Lillian's hand. "Here, we have collected enough money for you to go to Alexandria to rest."

A second friend stepped forward and said, "We will set up a roster to help Jennie with the children. You will see. When you come back, everything will be just as you left it."

Lillian looked around as her eyes filled with tears. "To think I have come halfway around the world to find such wonderful friends," she said. "Thank you from the bottom of my heart."

By that evening everything was arranged, and by the following afternoon, Lillian and baby Fareida were staying in a guest house in Alexandria. From her window Lillian had a wonderful view of the

Mediterranean Sea. Yet it was nearly impossible for Lillian to let her mind rest. She might physically be in Alexandria, but her heart was back in Assiout with Jennie and the children.

Chapter 8

Land Across the Nile

When Lillian returned from Alexandria two weeks later, everything was exactly as her neighbors had promised it would be. The children had been taken care of, and there was food in the pantry.

Lillian felt much stronger now and was able to go about her daily tasks with a new vigor. Most of the local people were beginning to understand that she and Jennie desired to raise orphaned children out of a sense of compassion. As a result they often gave Lillian small gifts of food or money.

Many subsistence farmers, or *fellahin*, as they were called in Egypt, lived in the countryside around Assiout. These farmers were also happy to help out the orphans, but they had no way to get their produce to the orphanage. Lillian soon realized that it was worth her while hiring a donkey and riding out into the countryside. As a six-foot-tall American woman with striking blue eyes, Lillian was hard to miss. The fellahin began to watch for Lillian, ready to load their vegetables and grain into the donkey's saddlebags. Lillian knew that sometimes it was a sacrifice for them to give at all, since many of the fellahin lived in poverty. She marveled at how cheerfully they gave. People around Assiout soon affectionately began to call Lillian "the woman on the donkey."

The help of the fellahin became more vital to Lillian as the brood at the orphanage multiplied over the next three years. By 1914 Lillian and Jennie were caring for eight children in the narrow, three-story house. The two of them set up a school for the children. They prayed and had Bible readings every morning and then gave English and Arabic lessons to the children. Lillian also bought paper and pens, which she used to write and illustrate her own textbooks for the children. She loved using her artistic abilities again and often smiled as she remembered how close she had come to being a newspaper artist. How grateful she was that the door to that job had been slammed firmly shut and she had obeyed the call to come to Egypt.

Since the house now served as a dormitory, dining room, and schoolhouse, it had become woefully small and inadequate to the task. Lillian began to pray about getting a larger house—a proper orphanage, where the children could run and play games and that had separate schoolrooms and a dining hall.

In August 1914 World War I began. Egypt sided with Great Britain in the war, and in November 1914 Great Britain declared Egypt a protectorate and assumed responsibility for protecting the Suez Canal. But for Lillian in Assiout, life went on as usual.

It was a Tuesday morning in July 1915 when Malik, one of Lillian's friends, came to visit. Malik was a government clerk, and he kept Lillian up-to-date on many of the happenings in the town. This particular day he looked pleased with himself.

"Mees Lillian," Malik said, "I have wonderful news. You know that half acre of land across the Nile, the land that you say would be a wonderful place for an orphanage. It is up for sale for fifty pounds!"

For a moment Lillian's faith deserted her. "Fifty pounds!" she exclaimed. "That's a fortune. Where would I get fifty pounds? That's the equivalent of two hundred fifty dollars."

Suddenly Lillian stopped speaking. Fifty pounds might be a fortune to her, but didn't the Bible say that God would supply all her needs? How would she get the money? In the same way she had gotten the money to meet her needs so far, by asking God to provide it for her.

"I'm sorry, Malik," she said. "I didn't mean to sound discouraging. What a wonderful opportunity this is. The children will have the kind of home they deserve. Think of it!" she said as her heart soared with faith. "We'll do it. Go tell the owner that I will buy the property. I'll have the money…" She hesitated for a moment. "I'll have the money a week from today."

Malik hurried off to deliver the message, and Lillian climbed the stairs to her room, where she sank to her knees and prayed. "Lord, show me what to do now. I need to have fifty pounds in a week, and I have less than one pound right now. It seems impossible, but I know that if You want the children to have this land, You will show me how to get it."

As she stood up, Lillian felt she had to do something, go somewhere. She hired a donkey and set off, not knowing where she was headed. "Show me the way, Lord," she prayed. "Show me the way."

The donkey had not taken Lillian far when she was reminded of an incident that had occurred a few days earlier. A wealthy businessman from a village three hours away had walked past her house. He seemed intrigued by the sight of all the children reciting their English lesson and had stopped to talk with Lillian, who explained her mission to him. As she spoke, the man had asked many questions and then handed her some money and his business card.

"Contact me if there is anything I can do to help you," the man had said as he left. It was these words that now rang in Lillian's ears. Perhaps this man visiting the house had not been a coincidence. Perhaps God had sent him along to meet this particular need. Lillian decided to visit the man and find out. After having spent four years in Egypt, Lillian knew that it was important to go about such a visit in the right way. This meant being formally introduced to the businessman by some other man he would respect.

As the donkey clopped along, Lillian thought about who could formally introduce her to the man. Her mind settled on the *mudir,* the governor of Assiout. Lillian had met him briefly, and she knew that he was interested in the work of her orphanage. How perfect it would be if the mudir would set up a meeting for her. She tugged on the reins and pointed the donkey down a side street. It was time to head for the governor's office.

The building that housed the mudir was just as grand and imposing on the inside as it was outside. Lillian was shown into the mudir's plushly furnished office, where she took a seat across from the large, inlaid desk behind which sat the mudir. After exchanging pleasantries for several minutes with the mudir, she plunged into telling him about the orphanage and the half-acre lot across the Nile. As she spoke, the mudir's eyebrows raised. He seemed impressed with all she was doing.

Finally Lillian got to the point of her visit. "I have no money, and I need fifty pounds to buy the lot across the river. A businessman in a nearby town told me to talk to him if I ever had any financial needs. I would like to visit him and talk about my need, and I would very much like your help in doing so. Could you arrange an appointment with the man for me?"

The mudir rocked in his chair for several moments and then nodded his head. "I would be delighted to do that," he said. "Would an appointment with the man at eleven o'clock tomorrow morning suit you?"

Lillian nodded.

"Very well. I shall contact him and make the arrangements. Do you have transportation to get to the town?"

"I have a donkey," Lillian replied cheerfully.

The mudir's face folded into a frown. "A donkey?" he asked incredulously. "An American woman rides around on a donkey! I can scarcely believe it."

"It is the best way I have to get around," Lillian replied simply. "I ride a donkey out into the countryside several days a week to collect the produce the fellahin donate to the orphanage," she continued.

"And no one has ever tried to attack you and rob you?" the mudir asked.

"No, never. God is my protector. He keeps me safe."

"Yes, as you say," the mudir said. "But a donkey—a donkey is the symbol of baseness and ridicule."

Lillian nodded. "But in the countryside the people do not worry about such symbols. They call me the woman on the donkey, and I don't think they mean it as an insult."

"Very well," the mudir said. "I will make the appointment for tomorrow, and you must leave early in the morning on your donkey to make it on time. I suggest you hire some donkey drivers to accompany you. This time of year the way can be quite treacherous."

"Thank you," Lillian said as she stood to leave the mudir's office. In accordance with protocol, her meeting with the businessman was now officially arranged and sanctioned.

As she rode back to the orphanage, Lillian said a prayer of thanks for receiving favor from the mudir. On the way home she stopped at a stable and hired two donkey drivers to accompany her on the trip the following day.

Very early the next morning the two donkey drivers were waiting for Lillian when she emerged from the house. A golden sliver of light was beginning to chase away the darkness as they rode out of Assiout.

It was nearing the peak of the flood season, when the Nile's water spread out beyond the river's banks, turning vast stretches of the surrounding low-lying countryside into swamps and lakes that were crisscrossed by submerged irrigation canals. As they rode out into the countryside, the donkey drivers had to take long diversions around the flooded land. By eight o'clock the morning sun beat down on them, and Lillian realized that all the diversions were eating up precious time. She began to fret about making it to the meeting with the businessman on time.

When they came to a vast lake, the two donkey drivers stopped and climbed off their donkeys. The two men looked at the water and then at each other as they talked quietly. Finally one of the men turned to Lillian and said, "The river is very high this year, Mees. This land should not be flooded as it is. We must ride out into the desert to get around it."

Lillian let out a deep sigh. "But we can't," she said. "We are already running late. We will not make it to the meeting if we have to go the long way."

To underscore what she was saying, Lillian leaped off her donkey, hitched up her long skirt, and waded out into the water.

"Mees Lillian, Mees Lillian, come back. It is dangerous," called the two startled donkey drivers.

"Look, the water is not deep. We can make it across," Lillian called back to them.

"No, come back. It is dangerous," they replied.

Lillian ignored their pleading as she took another step in the muddy water. But as she put her foot down, the bottom of the lake was gone! She sank straight down until the water covered her head. Moments later she surfaced, gasping for breath, drenched and covered from head to toe in silty mud. The two donkey drivers rushed forward to rescue her.

"You walked into an irrigation canal," they said as they guided her back to dry land.

Lillian was so embarrassed she could barely bring herself to look at the men. In her eagerness to get to the meeting, she had acted impulsively, ignoring the warning of her guides. She could easily have drowned. To make matters worse, her clothes were ruined, and she would have to find somewhere to change into the spare skirt and blouse she had packed in her donkey's saddlebag, using up more valuable time. She groaned, and they continued on their journey.

They came upon a small house nearby, where Lillian asked if she could change her clothes. Finally, dressed in clean, dry clothes, they got under way once again. As they headed out into the desert to get around the flooded expanse of land, Lillian despaired of making the meeting on time. But just as she was giving up hope, the donkey drivers managed to prod the animals into a bone-jarring gallop. Lillian held on tightly as her donkey's pace quickened. Before she knew it, they had detoured around the flooding and were approaching the town where the businessman lived.

At precisely eleven o'clock, Lillian pulled her donkey to a halt outside the businessman's house. She had made it on time after all. The man greeted her warmly and invited her inside. Lillian was soon in deep conversation with him, telling him about the plot of land across the Nile and how she would like to build a new and bigger orphanage on it. The businessman's eyes lit up as she spoke, and by the end of the meeting, he had given Lillian the fifty pounds she needed to purchase the land.

Lillian tucked the money deep into her handbag and thanked the businessman. In her mind the orphanage was as good as built. But as she was to find out, many challenges still lay ahead.

Chapter 9

Bricks

When the transaction to buy the plot of land was complete, Lillian had only a few piasters, or pennies, left over. They were a tiny beginning to paying for the buildings that would rise on the newly acquired land. Lillian reminded herself that the Bible said not to despise small beginnings. With that in mind, she turned her attention to what could be done with the piasters on hand. She soon had the answer. She could buy six wooden brick forms, and she and the children could start making bricks.

It was a hot day in September when Lillian and the children began their brick-making endeavor. Each form was divided into sections, which, when all were filled with mud, rendered twenty bricks. The mud to make the bricks came from mixing dirt dug up on the property with water from the nearby Nile. To this mud mixture was added manure and straw to ensure that the bricks dried hard and were strong. When all the ingredients were gathered, the boys climbed into the mixture and began to knead it with their feet. At first it was not easy to get the right consistency of mud, but eventually they learned the correct amount of water to add to make sure that the mud would dry into hard, strong bricks.

Once the mud was mixed, everyone gathered up handfuls of it and patted it into the forms. The forms were then left to dry for several days in the desert heat, which in the afternoons could reach 120 degrees Fahrenheit.

When she received some more money, Lillian bought additional forms, and soon hundreds of bricks were baking in the sun. Lillian surveyed the bricks with great satisfaction. This was how bricks had been made in the day of Moses and even Jesus, and it was how they were being made for the new orphanage.

Now that the bricks were baking in the hot sun, Lillian knew it was time to draw plans for the first building. She could not afford to hire an architect, and even if she could, she doubted he would be a lot of help. Egyptian people had no concept of orphanages, and Lillian knew in her mind exactly what she wanted. She set about transferring the picture in her head onto paper. The process of drawing exact plans took many long evenings, but slowly, night after night, the various elevations of the new building took form on paper. The dormitory would be built around a courtyard, where the children could play and Lillian could sit in the evenings. The walls would be at least two feet thick, as was the custom in Egypt to keep out the fierce summer heat, and each room in the building was designed to hold four beds.

Two weeks later the first batch of bricks were ready to be taken out of their forms. The bricks had turned from a deep brown to a gray color as they dried. In the meantime Lillian had been given enough money to hire a bricklayer to start work on the first wall of the girls' dormitory. His name was Misregee, and he was ready to start as soon as there were enough bricks.

Lillian showed Misregee the bricks the children had made. He turned a brick out of its form and examined it carefully. Finally he smiled. "Who would believe these children had not made bricks all their lives?" he said, turning to Lillian. "They are fine bricks."

"Wonderful, can you start tomorrow?" Lillian asked. "I will measure out the foundations and start the boys digging them. Then you can lay the bricks in the trenches."

Misregee shook his head. "These are good bricks for building walls, but for the foundation you need especially strong bricks. They cannot be made by hand; they must come from the factory. The amount you need will cost you three pounds."

Lillian gulped. Three pounds was a lot of money. Yet she heard herself say, "I will order them this afternoon, Misregee."

As soon as Misregee left, Lillian ran to a quiet spot at the corner of the property. She sank to her knees. "Lord, You know we need these bricks for a strong foundation. Please show me how You want to pay for them."

A peaceful assurance settled over Lillian as she went into Assiout to order the bricks from the brick factory. She did not have the money to pay for them, but she was sure the money would come.

Early the next morning Lillian set out on her round of fellahin villages. By now she had a routine, and each village knew when to expect her. The residents of a village would gather around to hear about the orphanage and other news from Assiout, and then they would contribute to Lillian whatever produce they could. This particular day Lillian's travels were supposed to take her to eleven villages, the last one being Kom Es Fat. However, it was still flood season on the Nile, and as Lillian approached the village, she found it surrounded by a ring of water two miles wide.

Wearily Lillian dismounted her donkey and looked across the muddy expanse of water. She wondered whether she should bother trying to make it to Kom Es Fat. With so much water, it would take a great deal of effort to get to one of the poorest villages on her route. But when Lillian thought of the friends she had met there on her previous visit and the chance to tell them that work was about to start on the first orphanage building, she knew she had to go there. She detoured to another village set on higher ground and there hired an old boat and an oarsman to take her to Kom Es Fat.

When she arrived, Lillian was rewarded with the smiles on many fellahin faces. The village leader stepped forward. "We are surprised to see you. We do not get many visitors when the Nile begins to rise, but welcome. We are glad you came. In fact, we have been talking about you for days, and we have gathered among us five pounds to help build your orphanage."

Lillian felt her eyes fill with tears. Never would she have expected this. She had no idea how these poor people had raised five pounds, but she appreciated their desire to help, as so many of her other Muslim friends had. Lillian now had enough money to pay for the bricks plus two pounds to buy supplies.

Lillian stayed as long as she dared with the people of Kom Es Fat before setting off in the boat again. She needed to get back across the watery expanse before nightfall. Before she climbed back into the boat, Lillian tied the five one-pound notes into a cotton bag that she wound around her wrist.

As the boat set out across the floodwater, the wind whipped up, and the boat seemed more rickety than ever to Lillian. The oarsman pulled hard on the oars, but he was barely making any headway against the growing, wind-stirred waves that now crashed over the bow.

Lillian hardly noticed the sun set, and within minutes of its going down they were in total darkness and being buffeted by waves and the swirling current. As they bobbed about, the moon broke through the clouds. Lillian let out a gasp. A huge wave was about to break on them. "Hold on," she yelled as she clutched the side of the boat.

The wave hit them with a thud, and water washed into the boat, but the boat did not sink. As soon as the wave passed, Lillian unraveled the cotton purse from her wrist and retied it more tightly. *If I drown,* she told herself, *when they find my body, I will still have the purse, and the bricks can be paid for.* In her shock she forgot to think about who else would take over the daunting responsibility of raising eight children and building an orphanage.

When the task of securing the money more tightly was complete, Lillian picked up the tin bucket that was floating in the bottom of the boat and began bailing the water. As she bailed, she kept a keen eye out for more waves and clung to the side of the boat with one hand.

The wind continued, and the muddy water drenched both Lillian and the oarsman. The boat was hit by one wave after another until Lillian was sure it would fall apart. Instead, it sprang a huge leak as several of the planks cracked apart. In the moonlight Lillian could see water spurting up near the stern. There was no way she could bail the water out as fast as it was coming in. Her heart beat fast as she realized the boat was about to sink. "Lord, help us," she yelled into the wind. At the same time the oarsman stripped off his shirt and stuffed it into the hole. The fountain stopped, but Lillian wondered for how long.

Wave after wave continued to swamp the boat. "Lord, I need help, I need help," Lillian sobbed, fearing the end was near. Then, without any warning, she felt a small nudge from under the boat, as if it were bumping into land. Lillian stopped sobbing and peered overboard. There was no land in sight, she was sure of that. She felt another nudge, slid to the side of the boat, and thrust her hand into the water. She felt something hard and round, like a broomstick. Excitement grew as she tried to imagine what was underneath the boat. Then suddenly she worked it out. Of course! The fellahin stacked cornstalks on top of their huts for safekeeping. Sometimes the stacks were twice as high as the hut they sat upon. The boat was bumping against one of these piles.

"This way," Lillian yelled to the oarsman, catching a glimpse of something more substantial sticking out of the water. Sure enough, it was the top of the pile of cornstalks. By now the boat was completely swamped and about to sink.

"Get out," the oarsman screamed.

Lillian did not hesitate for a second. She stood up and stepped out onto the cornstalk island. The oarsman was half a second behind her. As he climbed out, the boat sank from sight.

"Thank You, Lord, for providing this man-made island just in time," Lillian prayed. "But we can't stay on it with the river rising. Please help us to find a way back to shore."

Rain now began to beat down as Lillian and the oarsman clung to the cornstalk island. Lillian comforted herself with the fact that it must be sturdy to have lasted this long. Yet if the floodwater continued to rise, it would not matter how sturdy it was—the water would eventually wash it away.

Within minutes Lillian heard another sound, the swish of a passing boat. "Help! We're over here!" she yelled into the storm, but the boat slipped past them and into the night. Lillian redoubled her prayers, hoping that they were on some major water route. Much to her relief, a second boat came by a few minutes later. This time Lillian's shouts were heard, and the boat maneuvered toward them.

An hour later Lillian was reunited with her donkey. It was the middle of the night by now, and so she slept in a nearby hut. She set out for Assiout early in the morning. She was eager to get back and pay for the bricks so that Misregee could get to work.

Chapter 10

Losses and Gains

Several weeks later work on the first orphanage building was progressing well. One day, when she returned with the children from brick making at the new property, Lillian noticed a young man hanging around the house. He looked vaguely familiar to her, though she could not remember where she had seen him before. Lillian kept an eye on him as she prepared dinner. He seemed to be intently watching one child at play—Fareida. Then with a cry of alarm, Lillian realized who the man was. He had come to the Reverend Brelsford's mission house to fetch help for Fareida's mother when Fareida was an infant.

Lillian rushed outside and scooped four-year-old Fareida into her arms. Just then the man approached her. He fumbled in his pocket and pulled out a paper with an official stamp on it. Lillian hardly dared to look at it; she already knew what it was. She was sure that this man was Fareida's father and that he wanted his daughter back.

Lillian was overwhelmed by a sense of injustice as the man took the child she had raised from her arms and walked away. Fareida screamed, "Mama, Mama, don't let him take me away." But it was no use. Lillian did not have any paperwork that tied the child to her—only four years of caring for her.

Lillian cried for Fareida that night and for many nights afterward. She did not think she could be any more heartbroken until she received the terrible news that Fareida had died. It was almost too much for Lillian to comprehend. The little girl had been happy and in perfect health when her father took her away. All Lillian could do was ask God to soothe her aching heart and help her to continue her work with the children who remained.

By Christmas 1916 the orphanage building was completed. The boys had mixed the mud for all of the aboveground bricks, and the girls had kept Misregee and his helpers supplied with mortar. Lillian could not find the words to describe her joy as she and Jennie packed up their belongings and moved across the Nile to the new orphanage.

They moved just in time, too. The Great War was beginning to take a terrible toll on the people of Egypt. The British, who now controlled the country, demanded more and more army recruits. They made each provincial governor, or mudir, responsible for providing a set number of new soldiers. Stories began to be whispered about fellahin being kidnapped from their fields or forced from their homes and taken under escort to "volunteer" to serve in the British army.

As tragic as this was for the men involved, the women and children who were left behind often suffered more. Without their husbands and fathers they had no way to till their fields and produce food for themselves. Many families became desperate, but their pleas to the British government fell on deaf ears.

As a result of this situation, the number of orphans being brought to the orphanage climbed steadily. One morning in February 1917, one of the older girls came running into the room where Lillian was sewing clothes for the children.

"Mama, Mama," she said, "there is a woman with her children at the gate. She wants you to allow the children and her to stay here."

Lillian put down the pants she was hemming. "I will go and talk to her," she said, dreading the idea of telling the mother that her children could find shelter at the orphanage but she would have to find somewhere else to live.

When Lillian reached the gate, she found a pitiful sight—a young woman dressed in rags, with three small boys and a little girl, all with sunken cheekbones and dull eyes, clinging to her.

"I am Lillian Trasher. What can I do for you?" Lillian asked.

The woman looked up and, squinting at Lillian, said, "My husband is dead. The people in my village told me to take the children to the Lord's house. So we have walked here. Please, will you take them in, and me, too?"

Lillian shook her head. "We take only children here," she said as gently as she could. "You must go back to your village."

"But what point is that?" the young widow asked. "I am half blind, and I have no family there to help me. I have nothing and no one except my children."

Something inside Lillian broke as she looked at this sad family. She could not bring herself to insist the mother leave.

"Are you prepared to work around the place?" Lillian asked.

Tears filled the widow's eyes. "I would do anything to stay with my children. I can cook and clean and tend to babies."

"Very well," Lillian said, wrapping her arm around the woman's bony shoulders. "We will find a place for you here."

True to her word, the widow did what she could to help the orphanage run smoothly, and she was soon indispensable in the kitchen. Her children joined the other orphans, though they got to see their mother at mealtime.

Although Lillian had been reluctant to give shelter to the widow, she soon discovered what an asset extra hands could be around the place. When the next widow asked for a place to stay, Lillian readily agreed and soon started plans for a widows' dormitory.

On New Year's Day, 1918, Lillian counted fifty orphans and eight widows in her care. Although times were tough because of the war, each day there was food on everyone's plate and clothes on everyone's back.

By now the orphanage was running smoothly, and Lillian decided it was time to write a formal policy for running the home. She prayed about it for a long time before she came up with eleven points that would guide the running of the orphanage.

1. The Assiout Orphanage shall be a work of faith supported by freewill offerings.
2. All inmates—orphans or widows—shall be given free support.
3. There shall be no limit to the number of orphans accepted.
4. Relatives must sign a paper that they give the children to us until they are eighteen years old.
5. Relatives may visit the children anytime. Children may visit their relatives during holidays if they wish.
6. The orphanage shall not only clothe and feed its family but also give religious training and education and teach the trades of the land to each orphan as required.

7. Orphans who have relatives able to pay for their support shall not be accepted. There are boarding schools they can attend.
8. Each boy must give one year of free work to the orphanage, either after he has finished school or, if the orphanage should be in distress, he must stop school for one year, then return to finish his education.
9. Blind girls shall be accepted and taught to read Braille. (There is a home for blind boys in Egypt.)
10. As the customs of Egypt make it very hard for a girl who has been a servant to marry, our girls shall remain in the home until they marry. Those who do not wish to marry may remain in the institution as teachers and helpers.
11. Widows left with no support shall be accepted with their children. They will help with the younger children and do washing, mending, and cooking as to their ability and the need of the orphanage.

All the children helped out with the work around the orphanage. The older girls worked in the kitchen cooking and washing dishes. They also helped Lillian make and mend clothes and helped care for the babies. The boys worked outside tending the yard and making wooden chairs and leather goods that were sold in the market to raise money for the orphanage.

Around this time another American missionary, Sarah Smith, heard of Lillian's work and came to investigate it for herself. She was so impressed with what she saw that she decided to stay on and work with Lillian. She became housemother to the children.

As the months rolled by, more children and widows arrived at the orphanage. Lillian welcomed them all. With the ever-increasing number of residents, the orphanage facilities also grew, though there was a constant need for more dormitories and dining rooms.

With the passage of time, the older girls became adept at looking after the babies and toddlers with a minimum of supervision. Each teenage girl was put in charge of six smaller children during the daytime, and the small children came to look on their helpers as little mothers. Lillian was pleased with this arrangement because it meant that each small child had someone to bond with, someone who knew his or her personality and likes and dislikes. It made it feel more like a family than an institution.

The doctors at the Presbyterian hospital in Assiout did what they could to help out. They kept a special room just for the orphaned children. Up to six sick or malnourished children could be cared for at a time, and the hospital never charged Lillian for its services. Lillian would regularly visit the children in the hospital, and when a new sickly child arrived at the orphanage, she would take the plumpest, healthiest child home from the hospital and place the new arrival in the orphan ward for the doctors to care for. This arrangement worked well, and Lillian was grateful to have such expert medical care and the latest innovations available to her children.

On November 13, 1918, Jennie Trasher finally left Lillian to return to the United States. She had come to Egypt with the intention of staying just long enough to see her sister settled. Now eight years later she was finally going home to see to her rental properties and visit her parents. Lillian was sad to see her go. Jennie had been such a great help to her in establishing the orphanage.

The following day, November 14, brought wonderful news. The Great War was over! Germany had surrendered to Allied forces. The rejoicing in Egypt soon turned to anger, however, when the British did not loosen their grip on the country. When the war started, the British government had said it was taking over Egypt to protect the Suez Canal, but now that the canal did not need protecting, the British would not leave Egypt. Instead they passed laws that put more restrictions on the local people. Fearing an uprising, they ordered all Egyptians to hand their weapons over to the police. The Egyptians often carried guns for personal protection, and they hated the new law and grew angrier as the police tried to enforce it.

There were other problems, many of which Lillian was sympathetic to. One situation that she found particularly hard to accept was that no

Englishman could be tried for any crime he committed in Egypt, not even murder.

Slowly the anger escalated, until in March 1919 it boiled over. On March 15 Lillian unfolded the daily newspaper. The headlines blazed: "Six Egyptians Executed as Example." Lillian's heart dropped as she read the article, which reported that an Englishman had been practicing his rifle aim by shooting at a fellahin's pigeons. The Englishman had killed several of the birds, which meant that the fellahin and his family would have fewer eggs to supplement their already meager diet. Knowing that the Englishman could not be held accountable for killing his birds, the fellahin chased him off his property. Unfortunately the Englishman was not used to running, and he had a heart attack and dropped dead. When the British authorities heard this story, they decided to make an example out of it. After all, Egyptian men could not go around threatening Englishmen. So they ordered the police to shoot six fellahin—the pigeon owner and five of his friends—in front of their families.

It was almost too much for Lillian to believe. She was puzzled by the British response. Didn't they understand that Egypt was a powder keg waiting to be lit? Surely this horrible act would be the event that turned the seething anger of the Egyptians against the British into action. Time was to prove that Lillian's hunch was right. Yet even she could not imagine the peril that lay ahead both for Egypt and for her and her children.

Chapter 11

Rebellion

The day after the report in the newspaper of the atrocity, university students in a number of cities held demonstrations that quickly turned into riots. Other Egyptians joined them, calling for revenge and independence from Great Britain. Rebellion spread across Egypt. Rioting and looting broke out not only in the towns and cities but also out in the countryside. Whole villages were destroyed in the rampage. The telegraph and telephone lines, as well as the railway that connected Assiout with outlying areas, were sabotaged so that Lillian and all the other residents of the city were cut off from Cairo and the rest of Egypt.

Despite all that was going on in the country, Lillian kept her focus on the orphanage. As she went about her duties, she hoped that Assiout would be spared the mayhem that was occurring in other cities. However, this was not to be. Five days after the rebellion began, as twilight descended over the countryside, Lillian noticed something moving across the fields surrounding the orphanage. She went to investigate and was shocked to find a swarm of Egyptian men wielding guns and swords making their way toward the bridge that led to Assiout on the western bank of the Nile. The men had come to plunder the city. Assiout would not be spared the trauma of the rebellion.

Already shots were being fired back and forth across the river. Lillian raced to ring the bell, calling the children to gather in the courtyard. Her heart beat hard as she realized she had only a few minutes to get them to safety. About four hundred yards away from the orphanage on an adjoining property stood an old brick kiln. Despite being abandoned for many years, the kiln stood strong and was big enough for all the children to fit inside so that its thick, brick walls could protect them from the fighting.

When the children had gathered, Lillian told them, "Quickly, you older children, take the little ones you are in charge of and run for the kiln. Make sure no one is left behind."

With a flurry of activity, the children leapt to action. Soon a column of orphans was streaming through the darkness toward the old kiln. Lillian stayed behind to secure the house. Before she locked up, she made sure their cow was in the courtyard, where it would be more protected.

After locking the door to the orphanage, Lillian scooped her two small charges into her arms and, accompanied by one of the older girls carrying a baby, set off for the old kiln. By now it was pitch black, and from the sound of the gunfire, Lillian could tell the fighting was intensifying. As they ran, the girl carrying the baby tripped and fell forward. The baby girl she was carrying crashed to the ground. As the girl went to pick up the child, she let out a gasp. "Mama!" she exclaimed.

Lillian stopped to lend assistance. As she reached for the baby, she felt the blood. Shocked by the feel of warm blood, she squinted in the darkness to see where it was coming from. It was then that she saw the gaping gash beside the baby's right eye. The baby had struck her head against a sharp piece of metal protruding from the ground.

"Thank You, Lord, that the metal did not pierce her eye," Lillian prayed as she pressed a handkerchief against the gash to stem the blood flow. She picked up the child and again began running for the old brick kiln.

Finally everyone was safe inside the kiln. The blood flow from the baby's gash stopped, and Lillian handed the baby to one of the older girls to care for. It was then that Lillian counted the children and discovered that two toddlers were missing. Lillian risked her life to sneak back to the orphanage and retrieve the children who had been left behind, narrowly escaping two Egyptian men intent on killing her.

Once she and the two toddlers were reunited with the rest of the orphans within the thick walls of the kiln, Lillian gathered all the children close and offered a prayer of thanks to God for keeping them safe. Then she picked up her Bible and read to the children from Psalm 91: "A thousand shall fall at thy side, and ten thousand at thy right hand; but it shall not come nigh thee. Only with thine eyes shalt thou behold and see the reward of the wicked. Because thou hast made the Lord, which is my refuge, even the most High, thy habitation; there shall no evil befall thee, neither shall any plague come nigh thy dwelling."

When she had finished reading, Lillian asked Edward, one of the older boys, to read the verses in Arabic for those newer children who did not yet understand English.

When the reading was over, everyone settled down for a long night punctuated with the sounds of gunfire and bloodcurdling screams. Lillian took comfort in the verses she had just read and tried not to concern herself with what the marauding men might be doing to the orphanage. Somewhere in the early hours of the morning, Lillian finally drifted into a fitful sleep.

When Lillian awoke early in the morning, she cocked her ear. Was the gunfire over? Not hearing anything, she decided it was safe to slip outside for a look. She unbarred the door, stepped out into the sunlight, and walked toward the river's edge. Sharp pain ran up her leg from the ankle she twisted the night before, causing her to walk with a limp.

In the direction of Assiout rose huge billows of black smoke. Lillian gasped as she caught a full view of the city. The place was a smoldering ruin, a blackened wasteland. Lillian wanted to sit beside the river and weep for the people of Assiout, but she did not. She had 107 orphans to care for, and more would undoubtedly arrive as a result of the fighting.

With a heavy heart, Lillian turned back toward the orphanage. Bullet holes riddled the walls. With shaking hands she pushed open the door to the kitchen and went inside. Relief flowed through her as she realized the men who had surged around the orphanage during the night fighting and looting had left it untouched. She breathed a quick prayer of thanks and ran back to let the children out of the old kiln.

For the rest of the day everyone went quietly about his or her usual chores. Lillian was sure that the fighting was not over, but the best way to keep the children calm was to carry on the normal routine of the orphanage. Snippets of news filtered into the orphanage as the day progressed. The marauding men had swept through the countryside, burning or destroying as they went. All the neighboring farms had been decimated, including the farm of Said, one of Lillian's faithful supporters. Apparently he was the only one left on his land; everyone else had fled to Assiout. Lillian could only marvel that the men had not touched the orphanage with its supply of food and clothing. That evening Lillian made the decision to allow the children to sleep in the dormitories, as the fighting seemed to have moved farther to the south of Assiout.

At about seven o'clock the older girls were putting the babies and young children to bed, and the boys were doing homework in their rooms, when there was a loud knock at the door. Lillian went to the door expecting to find someone bringing an orphan he or she wanted her to take in. When she swung the door open, Lillian let out a piercing scream. A group of Egyptian men wielding clubs and swords burst into the house. They pushed Lillian roughly across the room and up against the far wall, where they pressed in around her. Before Lillian could think what to do, she heard a voice.

"Let her alone, let her alone," the voice yelled.

Lillian looked in amazement as her neighbor Said pushed his way through the press of burly men. When he got to the front, he stood between Lillian and the men and turned to address them.

"You men are not from here. You do not know who she is, but I do. This woman has taken in our Egyptian orphans and widows. She has given herself to serve them. She has done us nothing but good," he said.

A heavyset bearded man with angry, piercing dark eyes stepped forward. He pressed the tip of his sword against Said's belly. "If you do not get out of the way, you will be killed too," he snarled.

Said, who was barely half the size of the man with the sword, stood his ground. Lillian watched as he pulled himself up to his full height and stared at the man directly in the eyes. The man looked at Said and then at Lillian, who prayed a silent prayer, asking God to protect her and Said.

After what seemed like an eternity to Lillian, the man suddenly pulled his sword away from Said's belly, spun around, and stormed out of the orphanage. The other men followed him. As quickly as they had arrived, they were gone.

"Thank you, Said, thank you," Lillian said, grasping his hand.

Said said nothing. He just bowed and walked out of the orphanage. As Lillian watched him leave, she silently thanked God for His protection.

By Wednesday morning Lillian felt that the worst of the fighting and rioting was over. Realizing that she had not changed her clothes since Sunday, she decided it was safe enough for her to finally take a bath. She had just finished bathing when she looked out the window and saw a group of English soldiers marching toward the orphanage. She hurriedly pulled her hair into a bun and rushed out to greet them.

"Oh! How good it is to see you, boys!" she exclaimed. "Please come inside and have a cup of tea with me."

The sergeant stepped forward. "Thank you, Miss Trasher. We would be grateful for something to drink, but then you will have to leave with us."

"Leave?" Lillian replied. "Leave the orphanage?" She shook her head. "Surely you can see that I cannot leave the children. No, I won't leave."

Chapter 12

A Sad Goodbye

"There is no choice, children or not," the sergeant told Lillian. "The general has ordered that all foreigners who are not government employees must leave tomorrow. In fact, there are two steamers moored in the river waiting to take everyone to Cairo. You will be safe there."

"Cairo?" Lillian repeated. "Safe in Cairo? But I have been safe here." She swept her hand across the buildings. "Surely you have noticed that not a thing has been touched, whereas all the neighbors' homes have been ransacked. Besides, more than one hundred Egyptian children call me Mama, so I am not a foreigner."

The sergeant smiled comfortingly at Lillian. "Of course, Miss Trasher. I have heard of the work you do here, but I am not the one ordering you to leave. You may go and plead your case to the general if you wish. He has set up office in the Assiout Hotel. But you cannot stay here tonight. I have orders to escort you to the boat."

Lillian groaned. She could not imagine being separated from the children and the widows who depended on her for their livelihood. Yet she knew that the sergeant had orders to follow and he would not leave without her.

"Very well," she said. "The children and I will go to Assiout and spend the night there. In the morning I will visit the general and ask for his help. Will you allow some of your soldiers to remain here and watch over the orphanage while we are gone?"

"Most certainly," the sergeant replied. "Now, how about that cup of tea before we set out?"

It took two hours to assemble all the children, along with clothing, food, and supplies for the stay in Assiout. Lillian planned to ask the hospital to house the girls and babies overnight and the American school to shelter the bigger boys.

With a heavy heart, Lillian set out for the city, holding Leila, one of the smallest children, in her arms. It was an hour's walk down the road across the bridge over the Nile and into Assiout. The older children knew why they were making the trek, and the sobbing started before they had passed through the orphanage gates. Soon the entire line of children was in tears, along with the orphanage doorkeeper and the widows. Lillian was emotionally exhausted, and tears flowed down her cheeks.

"How can this be, Lord?" she prayed as she walked. "Have You led me to look after these people for nine years only to allow me to be ordered to leave? Surely You know how much these children mean to me."

She looked down at baby Leila snuggled contentedly in her arms. Could it be only a month ago that a neighbor came to the orphanage with the child? "I was coming from the city and walking across the big Nile bridge," the neighbor had told her. "When I got to the middle of the bridge, I saw a blind man just as he was about to throw this baby into the river. I rushed up to him and grabbed the baby and said, 'You wicked man. You must not throw a living baby into the water.' And the blind man replied, 'I have no place to keep her. Now that you have stopped me, she is yours.'"

Now Leila was a thriving child with a secure future—or at least it had been until the British general ordered Lillian to leave.

Lillian pondered how ironic it would be if, after all the times they had been perilously short of food and money, it was the British government that was responsible for the closing of the orphanage.

Somehow the sobbing crowd reached Assiout, and Lillian settled everyone in for the night. She stayed in the hospital with the girls and the babies for what was the worst night of her life. Nothing she had ever experienced came close to the anguish of knowing that in the morning she could be separated from her children. It was like losing Fareida and her subsequent death all over again times 107.

The sobbing of the children made it impossible for anyone to sleep, though Lillian knew she could not sleep anyway. She cried until she feared she was going mad. Then sometime around three in the morning, Lillian felt calm come over her. She lay on her cot, her mind at rest for the first time in days.

"Lord, is there something You want to say to me?" she prayed.

A question implanted itself in her mind. *If you have to leave, why go to Cairo?*

If not Cairo, then where? she countered.

A second thought came to her. *Why not return to the United States? There is nothing you can do in Cairo, and if you return to America, you will be able to raise money for the orphanage and get more Christians to pray for you.*

Lillian sat up astounded at how excited she felt. Just ten minutes ago she had been sobbing her heart out at the thought of leaving her children. Now she felt that God had a reason for her to leave. What a difference that made! She smiled to herself. "Yes, Lord. If You are sending me, I will gladly return to the United States."

Suddenly Lillian's mind was flooded with plans. It was as if somewhere deep inside she had been thinking of this for weeks. There was no need for the orphanage to close just because she left. She could still play a vital role by taking on the responsibility of supplying the orphanage with money, just as she had done for nine years. Her faithful assistant Zackeah Nashid could easily take care of the daily logistics by himself, and Oma, one of her most capable and reliable widows, could take charge of the children.

The following morning Lillian went to see the general. Even though she pled her case to him, she was not surprised when he turned her down. She was now convinced that God was calling her back to the United States.

Still, it was no easy task disentangling herself from the children and climbing aboard the *Victoria*, the river steamer that would take her to Cairo. She knew the children had made a pact with each other not to cry so as not to make parting with their Mama any more difficult than it had to be. However, the lips of the children trembled and tears danced in their eyes as Lillian kissed each child goodbye and promised to return as soon as possible.

Lillian climbed the gangplank onto the steamer with many other foreigners. Most of them lugged heavy suitcases and parcels, but not Lillian. All she had with her was a well-worn brown bag, the same one she had arrived with in Egypt nine years before. And the bag was not even full. All it contained was a change of clothes, her Bible, and a pen and some writing paper. These items accounted for virtually everything Lillian owned.

From Cairo Lillian made her way to Alexandria, where she caught a steamer bound for New York.

The trip through the Mediterranean and across the Atlantic Ocean was swift, and six weeks after leaving Assiout, Lillian found herself once again on American soil. Now she really felt like a foreigner. So much had changed in the years she had been away. Dresses were now shorter, with dropped waists and no sleeves. Motor cars were everywhere, clogging city streets, and the young people listened to music that could only be described as jaunty. Their youthful faces made Lillian realized that she was no longer a young person—she was now a thirty-one-year-old missionary with over one hundred people in her care.

After a brief stay in New York City visiting friends, Lillian headed for California to visit Jennie. Jennie was the only person in the United States who understood the kind of life Lillian lived. Since Lillian's father's death, Lillian's seventy-one-year-old mother had moved in with Jennie. The three of them enjoyed a wonderful reunion.

A week into her stay with Jennie, Lillian was invited to a church belonging to the Assemblies of God, a new Pentecostal church that had been founded five years before, in 1914. The moment Lillian walked through the door of the church, she felt at home. For the most part the people were from farming or blue-collar backgrounds, and they had a vitality about them and a complete trust in God that drew Lillian like a magnet. Before long Lillian joined the denomination and went on a nationwide speaking tour that included many Assemblies of God churches.

Although the denomination's leaders made it clear that they could not take on the financial burden of the orphanage, many individuals gave what they could to help Lillian. In addition the Women's Missionary Council promised to collect old clothes and box them up for the orphan children. Other people pledged to pray for Lillian every day. To Lillian prayer was just as important as the material goods she was offered.

During her national tour Lillian was able to regularly send money back to Egypt, and by the time the tour was finished, she had also put a tidy sum of money into a bank account.

Lillian kept in touch with Zackeah Nashid by mail, and in the spring of 1920 she decided it was time to go home to Egypt. By now the political situation in the country had settled down and foreigners were allowed to return to Assiout.

It was a wonderful day for Lillian when she once again walked through the gates of the orphanage. Children squealed with delight as they recognized her, and she was soon engulfed in hugs and kisses. Some children hung back. They were the new orphans who had only heard of their legendary "Mama."

Zackeah and Oma had done an excellent job in Lillian's absence. Barrels of clothing and blankets—gifts from her new friends in the United States—were waiting for Lillian.

The dormitory rooms were now so crowded that some of the children were sleeping four to a bed.

Lillian set out to build another dormitory. The older boys made the bricks as they had done before, and they were also able to help the professional bricklayers with their work. All this helped to keep building costs down. As soon as the new dormitory was completed, it filled up with children, and another dormitory was planned.

By now Lillian, or Mama Trasher, as everyone called her, was well known in Egypt. In 1921 the sultan came to visit her. One hundred fifty children were now living at the orphanage. The sultan was so impressed with them that he gave Lillian fifteen hundred pounds to use as she pleased. The money went straight into the building fund. Lillian had expanded her vision to include vocational buildings for the boys, and bit by bit, woodworking and metalworking rooms were built and equipped with the latest machinery. Some of the older boys were soon competent enough to take on many of the maintenance projects around the orphanage.

Since the political situation in Egypt was more stable, English and American tourists were starting to trickle back into the country. They wanted to see the pyramids and the sphinxes and the tombs of the pharaohs. Happily for Lillian, many of them wanted to take a leisurely boat tour down the Nile as far as Luxor. The new tourist boats always stopped at Assiout to refuel, and the passengers were encouraged to disembark and walk around the town. After seeing several of these tours pass through, Lillian came up with the idea of printing fliers to invite the tourists to visit the largest orphanage in Egypt. Many of them took up the offer, and Lillian made many new friends who promised to support the orphanage in one way or another.

The work continued to grow until, in 1924, three hundred children were living in the orphanage. It cost about one thousand dollars a month to feed and clothe them all. To help defray some of the costs, the older girls made the clothes for the children. Lillian insisted on cutting the pieces to be sewn from the cloth herself. The cloth was expensive, and she knew how to get the maximum number of garments from each bolt of fabric. The women of the Assemblies of God in the United States also sewed clothes for the children and shipped them to Assiout.

By now every available inch of the orphanage land had been built on, and Lillian began to pray earnestly for the money to buy the property adjacent to the orphanage on the south. The land was fertile, and Lillian could already envision the children working in the vegetable garden and cows grazing on the grass. How wonderful it would be to have a regular supply of fresh milk for the babies.

The answer to Lillian's prayer came in an unusual way. A number of wealthy Egyptian families heard of the need and collected twenty-six hundred pounds among them. They used the money to buy the two and one-half acres of land. When they presented the deed to the property to Lillian, she was too overcome to speak. Every new square foot of land represented the opportunity to welcome more destitute children into the orphanage.

Once again Lillian set out to raise money to buy bricks and pay the laborers for the new dormitories.

As the orphanage continued to grow, so did the need for money to cover the daily operating costs. To raise this money, Lillian often set out on her donkey to visit various wealthy families. She would describe the work of the orphanage and ask each family if it would like to help financially.

One particular day Lillian needed seventy-five pounds to cover various necessities at the orphanage. As usual, she climbed onto her donkey early in the morning and rode off to visit a wealthy family that lived on the outskirts of Assiout. When Lillian arrived at the house, she learned that the man of the house was not yet out of bed. Lillian decided to return to the house at noon. When she arrived the second time, she learned that the man had gone out. At three in the afternoon Lillian returned to the house a third time. This time she learned that the man of the house was too busy to see her just then. Lillian decided to wait until he was free. A servant showed her into the drawing room, where she sat down on a straight-backed, wooden chair.

After an hour the man had still not seen her, and Lillian felt her spirits beginning to deflate. When one of the servants passed through the drawing room, she looked at Lillian and said, "If I had the money, I would give you what you need."

When the servant had gone, Lillian realized that she was not wanted at the house and that rather than being busy, the man of the house was avoiding her. A sense of abandonment swept over Lillian, and she began to weep. In her despair she sank to her knees beside the chair.

"I cannot do this anymore, Lord," she prayed. "I'll take care of the children. You provide the money. I cannot go about on my donkey begging for money and still have energy to tend to the children."

Her sobbing subsided, and Lillian knelt quietly for several minutes. Then she added to her prayer, "Lord, will You please send me seventy-five pounds today? That way I will know that You have heard my cry and that I am walking in Your way."

With that Lillian rose to her feet, left the wealthy Egyptian family's home, and headed back to the orphanage on her donkey. When she reached the orphanage, Lillian learned that in her absence an Egyptian friend had come to visit her. Not finding her in, the friend had left a note and a small container, which Oma now handed to Lillian.

Lillian opened the note and read. The note explained that the friend's daughter had become engaged and the family wanted to share their joy with Lillian. Lillian opened the container that had been left with the note. Inside she found a wad of pound notes. As she counted them, Lillian discovered that the container held not seventy-five pounds but two hundred!

"Thank You, Lord," she prayed. "I will not go out on my donkey begging for money again. Indeed, I will spend my time caring for the children and trust You to send the money to feed, clothe, and educate them."

Chapter 13

Unexpected Blessings

Lillian heard the shrill whistle of the luxury steamer on the Nile. Instinctively she gathered up a pile of brochures describing the orphanage and headed for town. She found the steamer tied up at the dock alongside the Nile. She climbed aboard and began to hand out her brochures.

"Come and see the largest orphanage in Egypt, which is run by faith," Lillian told people.

No one seemed very interested, so Lillian made her way over to a table on deck where a group of people sat sipping tea. Again she invited the people to visit the orphanage. No one spoke to her or even looked up. She repeated her invitation. This time the young man sitting closest to where she stood turned to Lillian, fixed his eyes on her, and then blew cigarette smoke in her face. "I am on holiday. The last thing I want to see is a group of orphans," he snapped before turning back to the table.

Lillian heard a snicker go around the table. She turned and walked away. In all her years of visiting the steamers and inviting people to visit the orphanage, she had never been treated so rudely. Dejected, Lillian walked along the deck wondering whether anybody aboard was interested in visiting the orphanage. She was just about to give up when she heard a voice behind her. "May I have one of your brochures?" the voice asked.

Lillian turned to see a pretty young woman with reddish blonde hair. The woman's face was warm and encouraging, and a smile curled around the corners of her mouth and eyes as she took the brochure from Lillian.

The woman quickly read the brochure and then said to Lillian, "I am Lady Inskip of Scotland. I would very much like to see your orphanage. May I come and visit this evening?"

"You would be most welcome," Lillian replied, smiling back.

Lillian spent the rest of the day cleaning and tidying, and by early evening everything was spic-and-span. Shortly after seven o'clock there was a knock at the door. It was Lady Inskip. A man about thirty years older, sporting a mop of the same reddish blonde hair, accompanied her.

"Good evening, Miss Trasher," Lady Inskip said. "Allow me to introduce my father, Lord Maclay."

Lillian reached out and shook the man's hand before inviting them in. She was not used to addressing titled visitors and was unsure what to call them. Finally she asked.

"My dear Miss Trasher, you may address me any way you wish," Lord Maclay said. "Any titles I might have shrink to insignificance compared to the nobility of your character and work."

Lillian felt her face turn red with embarrassment at the compliment.

Proudly Lillian showed her guests around the orphanage. They seemed most impressed with all she was doing, and before they left, Lord Maclay handed her twenty pounds and promised to do all he could to support her work. And he was true to his word. When the river steamer arrived back in Cairo after leaving Assiout, Lord Maclay sent another hundred pounds to Lillian to support her work with the orphans. Lillian was overjoyed.

Not long after Lord Maclay and Lady Inskip's visit to the orphanage, a group of wealthy Egyptian women once again banded together. This time it was not to buy land but to buy a brand new automobile for Lillian. It did not take Lillian long to learn how to drive the car, and soon the car was a familiar sight around Assiout and the surrounding villages. Lillian's donkey-riding days were over. She now had a comfortable leather seat to sit in when she traveled, not the bony back of an animal.

One way or another, money came in to keep the orphanage running. On one occasion a rich Egyptian man came to tour the orphanage. It was a Tuesday morning, and the man had heard about Lillian's work with the orphans and wanted to see it for himself. After the regular tour, he asked Lillian where all the food was stored.

"When we have it, we keep it in the storeroom behind the kitchen," she replied, "but at the moment it's empty."

"Do you mean to say you have no food for tomorrow?" he sputtered.

"Well, yes," Lillian replied.

"How awful!" he exclaimed. "Will you be able to sleep tonight?"

One of the older orphan girls who was standing nearby laughed out loud.

The man swung around to confront her. "Young lady, this is no joke. She says there is no food for tomorrow, and there are hundreds of mouths to feed.

The teenager spoke up. "Why, Mama never has any food for tomorrow, and she never loses sleep over it!"

"Is this true?" the man asked. "Has this happened before?" He stopped for a moment to study Lillian's face. "What will you do if money does not come in to buy food?"

Lillian smiled. How wonderful it was to not only tell people that God provided for them but also show them. "During all the years the orphanage has been in operation, the children have never missed a meal," she said. "Certainly there have been times when our faith was tested, but God has never failed us yet, and I don't expect He will now."

Lillian watched as the visitor tried to take in what she had said. She knew it was amazing—a lone foreigner taking care of over five hundred children and widows without a steady source of income. It did seem ridiculous without God, she reminded herself.

Early the following morning the man returned to visit Lillian. "When I left the orphanage," he told her, "I went to a nearby village on business. I mentioned to the man where I had gone to visit and that I had just come from here. He handed me this and asked me to give it to you the next time I saw you." With a look of disbelief, the man pulled one hundred pounds from his pocket. "I suppose you have food for another day after all."

Lillian smiled. "The Lord feeds the sparrows and clothes the lilies in the fields, and He looks after the widows and the orphans."

"I cannot dispute that," the man replied. "It's remarkable, quite remarkable."

Two weeks later Lillian's faith was again tested. This time it was by a widow who came to the gate of the orphanage. Her name was Toffa. As Lillian greeted her, she learned that the woman had walked four miles with her three children to get to the orphanage. She was also partially blind and pregnant with her fourth child.

"My husband has been out of work for eight months," she told Lillian, "and we have nothing at all to eat. Can you help us, please?"

Taking compassion on the desperate woman, Lillian gave her five pounds from the orphanage funds, a dozen loaves of bread, some rice, sugar, and six bars of soap. Lillian then loaded Toffa and her children into the car and drove them to town, where she bought them tomatoes, potatoes, butter, and several pounds of meat. She then took them to their ramshackle hut outside of town.

On her way back to the orphanage, Lillian stopped at the grocery store in Assiout to purchase some items needed at the orphanage. Lillian told the store clerk that she needed a basketful of rice and a box of sugar. Before the clerk went to get the items, Mr. Badeer, the store owner, emerged from the back room. "Get her a large sack of the best rice, a large box of sugar, and one hundred pounds of soap," he told the clerk.

"No, no," Lillian said. "I can't possibly afford all that, and besides, I don't need soap."

"Take it. It is my gift to you. Keep it until you need it," Mr. Badeer said.

"Thank you for your generosity, and may God bless you," Lillian said as she left the store.

On the drive back to the orphanage, Lillian thanked God for providing for them. She had given Toffa several handfuls of rice, and now she had a whole sack of the best quality rice. She had given away several pounds of sugar, and now she had the biggest box of sugar Mr. Badeer carried in his store. And she had given Toffa six bars of soap, and now she had one hundred pounds of it.

As if that were not enough, later that evening Dr. Aziz, a friend from Assiout, arrived at the orphanage to deliver fifty pounds that a wealthy businessman had given to him for the orphanage. Lillian had given Toffa five pounds, and now she had fifty pounds to replace it!

Not long after this incident, another person arrived at the orphanage. This time it was an old man Lillian had not seen before. By the look of him, she supposed him to be very poor. He arrived when Lillian was in the middle of showing a group of tourists from a Thomas Cook Nile Tour around the orphanage. As she showed the tourists around, Lillian quietly prayed that God would touch some of their hearts to give financially to the orphanage, since the orphanage was once again short of money.

When Lillian spotted the old man, she left the group for a moment and went to invite him to sit inside.

"No, not now," he said. "I can see you are busy."

Lillian left him at the gate and continued with the tour. When it was over, the tourists thanked Lillian for her time and contributed thirteen pounds to the orphanage. While Lillian was grateful for it, she knew that it would not go far.

As she walked back toward the main orphanage building, the old man walked up to greet Lillian. "Come in," she said. "Would you like to have tea with me?"

The old man nodded and followed her into the drawing room. When they were both seated, the man sheepishly handed Lillian a crumpled bill. It was fifty pounds! "This is for your orphanage," he said.

Lillian had to stop herself from laughing out loud as she thought of all those rich tourists giving thirteen pounds and this one poor, old Egyptian man giving her nearly four times that much. *God's ways are not our ways!* Lillian chuckled to herself.

On the night of April 7, 1927, a most unusual event occurred at the orphanage. Lillian had called the children and widows together for the usual devotional time, during which she read to them from the Bible and they then all prayed. Lillian read a passage from the Bible and had begun to explain its meaning to the children when she became aware of sniffles and sobs around the room. Suddenly children began to get down on their knees and confess their sins aloud to God and ask Him to forgive them and make them new people inside. Soon the sound of prayer and confession drowned out Lillian.

The meeting went on long into the night, and when the children were sent to bed, they continued to pray in groups in their dormitory rooms or alone lying on their beds. The following day more prayer and confession of sin continued. This pattern went on for five days, and during that time the lives of many of the children in the orphanage were completely turned around. Children asked other children to forgive them for the way they had treated them, and a renewed sense of love and acceptance of one another spread through the orphanage.

Not content to just stay at the orphanage and enjoy the wonderful experience, the children asked to be allowed to go into Assiout and the surrounding countryside to share with others what had been happening at the orphanage. Lillian agreed, and many Egyptians in the small villages heard the gospel message preached by the children. The children's joy was infectious, and as a result, many people became Christians.

Lillian had given much in the course of caring for the physical needs of the children in the orphanage, and she was delighted by what was now happening. Her years of praying for the children and sharing the gospel message with them had come to fruition. In a letter back to the United States, she wrote, "I have wonderful news to tell you. God has given us one of the most wonderful revivals I have ever seen in my life. The power of God is sweeping the orphanage like a mighty flood, like a terrific fire, or like I imagine it will be at the great Judgment Day. Hundreds of children are on their faces screaming out to God for mercy, some shouting for joy and rejoicing in the marvelous newfound blessing."

Chapter 14

Blessing and Loss

It was Thanksgiving Day, November 1930, and Lillian sat at her desk trying to recall what Thanksgiving Day had been like in the United States. It all seemed like a distant dream now. Her heart belonged to Egypt; she even thought in Arabic most of the time. With a light heart she picked up her pen and started writing a newsletter to send home to the Assemblies of God churches.

> Many times God not only sends help but sends the very thing we are in need of. Two weeks ago, the woman who has charge of the little boys' nursery came to me saying that the children's mattresses were torn and so badly worn through that some of the children

were nearly sleeping on the springs. I told her that I was very, very sorry, but I had no money at all and that I thought all last year's cotton was used up. I told her that they would have to pray for God to send help. I sent for the woman in charge of the bedding. As we were all three talking about it, and as she was telling them that there was not a bit of cotton left from last year, I looked out the window and saw a large motor truck drive up piled with huge sacks of cotton (worth about fifty dollars), a gift to the orphanage.

To encourage herself and the orphanage staff through the many hard times, Lillian often quoted the verse, "Hitherto hath the Lord helped us." Somehow the things that the orphans needed the most always showed up in the nick of time. Just three days after she began writing the newsletter, Lillian added another entry to it.

Some of the girls came to the woman in charge of the soap, asking for their allowance. The woman said, "We have none." The same day this woman's mother, who was ill, had sent for some rice. The storeroom supply was down to only a few handfuls. About five o'clock a car drove up with all kinds of gifts piled in it, large and small. There were six five-gallon tins of butter, six tins of cheese, a large sack of soap, a sack of rice, two and a half boxes of sugar, and many smaller things, worth perhaps over one hundred dollars in all. A woman had died four months previous, and before her death, she had asked her relatives to please send the things in her storeroom to the orphanage.

These provisions became even more precious as money and supplies from the United States began to dwindle. The world was in the grip of the Great Depression, and money was scarce everywhere. At the same time more children than ever poured into the orphanage. Lillian became especially attached to one of these children, a tiny baby boy who was found near the railway track on a freezing morning. The boy apparently had been lying in the open all night, naked and alone. A carpenter at the American College in Assiout had found him on his way to work, and as soon as Lillian heard about the baby, she urged the carpenter to bring him straight to her. The boy arrived at the orphanage at eight o'clock in the morning, still naked but wrapped in an old bran sack. He was covered with sand and dirt from being outside on such a cold, windy evening.

Lillian cast an experienced eye over the baby and decided he was not more than twelve hours old. She knew she had to get his body temperature up if he was to survive. She poured three large pans of hot water into a bath and began to wash him and warm him at the same time. The dirt and sand were soon rinsed off him, and his body relaxed as

Lillian sang softly to him. "I think we shall call you Faheem abd Alla," she said as she bathed the child. "That means 'Understanding, the servant of God.'"

When all of the sand had sunk to the bottom of the bath, Lillian carefully lifted Faheem out of the water, dried him, and then dressed him. She filled two hot water bottles and tucked them into his blanket to keep him warm. She then fed him a bottle of warm milk. Even though Faheem had a rough start to life, he thrived from the first day at the orphanage. Lillian was delighted to see him growing strong and happy.

As the depression dragged on, Lillian continued to be amazed at how the orphanage survived. In 1927 the annual income at the orphanage was nearly twenty-five thousand dollars. By 1933 it had plummeted to under fifteen thousand dollars. But that year it was not the falloff in money that became Lillian's greatest worry but something much worse.

It was early June when Lillian first heard the chilling news from Port Said, where a Swedish orphanage was located. A missionary at this orphanage had spanked one of the orphans in her care, an eight-year-old girl. The girl promptly ran away and reported the spanking to the police. She told the police officers that she had been beaten for refusing to become a Christian.

Within hours the accusation was the talk of Egypt. People asked, "How could Christians be trusted to raise Muslim children? Don't Muslim children deserve to be in orphanages where they are taught their own faith?

The Swedish missionary was expelled from Egypt, but that was not enough to satisfy many Muslim Egyptians. They demanded that *all* Muslim children be removed from Christian care and put into Muslim orphanages. Worse, some Muslim leaders were stirring up ways to harass the missionaries who were working among Egyptians from the Coptic Christian tradition, hoping to drive all missionaries out of the country.

It was not long before Lillian received the visit she dreaded. A government official stood at the door. Lillian invited him in, and he got straight to the point.

"Do you have a girl named Pauline here?" he asked.

"Yes," Lillian replied. "I have a Pauline who is twenty-two years old. Is that the one you mean?"

The official nodded. "The governor has a report that you are paying Pauline and her younger sister one dollar and fifty cents a month to convert to the Christian faith. We believe you have gone so far as to baptize her. Do you have anything to say in the matter?"

Lillian grasped her hands behind her back so the official would not see how much they were shaking. She took a deep breath and tried to explain Pauline's situation.

"She came to us when she was four years old. A soldier found her wandering alone in the desert and took her to the American hospital. When she was six, she ran away from the hospital and came here. I telephoned the hospital and told them where she was, but they said I could keep her if I wanted. She was not sick, and she really didn't belong there. She fit in here right away, and we had no idea whether she was Coptic or Muslim. When she was fourteen, she asked to be baptized, and we did so."

Lillian paused for a moment and offered a quick prayer. *God, please help this man hear what I am saying. The lives of seventy of my children depend on it.* She continued talking to the official.

"About a year ago Pauline wanted to find her family, so I made inquiries, and we were able to find them. They were a Muslim family. The father was dead, but the mother was still alive, and Pauline had several brothers and sisters. They were all desperately poor, and so the mother asked if we could take another daughter, Miriam, into the orphanage and raise her the same way we had raised Pauline. We agreed to do this, and Pauline asked that we put her mother on a charity list we keep here at the orphanage. Every month we have many widows and old people to whom we give small amounts of money. We decided to give Pauline's mother a dollar fifty to help with food for the other children. There are no strings attached to the money."

Having explained the situation as best she could, Lillian studied the official's face. It was impossible to tell whether or not he was sympathetic to her cause, or whether he even believed her.

"I will need to see the charity list, and I will report what you have said to the governor," the official replied.

"What then?" Lillian asked.

He shrugged his shoulders. "Then we shall see what the governor has to say."

Tensions continued to build over the following two weeks. Muslims collected thousands of dollars to build new orphanages so that the orphans would not have to go to Christian ones. In the midst of this fervor, some churches were broken into and preachers beaten, and one convent was partially destroyed. Meanwhile the governor sent several officials to inspect every aspect of Lillian's orphanage. The officials went through the accounting ledgers and held interviews with the orphans. They questioned the widows and the teaching staff and took copies of all the booklets Lillian had produced.

Finally, on July 5, the governor sent for Lillian. The news was not good. Although he thanked her for the work she had done, he had made his decision: All the Muslim children in the orphanage were to be removed in ten days' time. Lillian trembled as she heard the news. Seventy of her children were being taken away at once! It was almost more than she could bear.

Ten days later government officials arrived to take away the Muslim children. Lillian watched helplessly, her heart breaking within, as the children were loaded onto two buses. Many of them were leaving the only home they had ever known.

Much to the irritation of the officials, Lillian insisted on kissing each child goodbye. Hennana, a six-year-old girl who was blind and had a crooked leg and twisted arm, was escorted to the bus. She had been in the orphanage since she was a few days old, and Lillian hated to see her taken away, because she needed such special care. As she bent to kiss Hennana goodbye, one official pulled Lillian aside.

"Why do you kiss her? Look at her. What good is she? You can keep her," the official said with a scowl.

"Thank you," Lillian said politely as she guided Hennana away from the line of children being loaded onto the buses. At the same time she whispered a prayer of thanks to God. She was sure the official had been trying to insult her by leaving Hennana behind, but in truth Hennana was the most needy child and therefore the one Lillian would have chosen to stay behind if she had been given that choice.

Pauline, who was legally an adult, was also allowed to stay behind at the orphanage. She and Lillian stood side by side watching, tears streaming down their faces, as the buses drove away from the orphanage.

Although the Muslim children were gone, they cried so much for "Mama" that the officials asked Lillian to visit them and calm them down. It broke Lillian's heart to see them so sad, but she did what she could to settle them in and promised that when they were old enough to leave the Muslim orphanage, they were welcome to visit her in Assiout.

Along with the heartache of losing the children, Lillian had moments of joy. By now many of her older "boys" (some of them were young men in their late teens and early twenties) were going out into the surrounding countryside to preach. A month after the children were taken, Lillian visited the village of Sheik Soufi, a place she had never been before. One of her boys had been preaching there and wanted her advice on how to open a school and mission. When Lillian entered the village, she was drawn to a derelict building with four walls and a caved-in roof.

"Who does this belong to?" she asked a village elder.

"A long time ago one of the men in the village deeded it as a church, and a preacher from the Presbyterian college used to come every Sunday morning. Now the man is dead, and the preacher does not come."

"How long ago was that?" Lillian asked.

"About seventeen years ago," another man replied.

"Well, that is seventeen years too long to go without the Word of God!" Lillian exclaimed. She was so proud that one of her boys was going to bring the gospel back to these people and that there was already a building waiting for him to use, albeit with some needed repairs.

On her way home, Lillian visited the village of Deir Busra, where another one of her boys was supervising the building of a mission school.

Lillian was overjoyed to think that her children were turning into evangelists. That night she wrote in her diary, "We hope to put a new top on the old church and open a school and mission there this summer. How we hope the little boys and girls of today will get what their fathers lost so long ago."

When the Muslim children were taken away, the total number of children in the orphanage dropped for the first time ever, going from seven hundred at the beginning of 1933 to six hundred fifty by year's end. In some ways Lillian was grateful that the children had not been replaced right away. She had always struggled with getting food on the table, and with the depression dragging on, the need for provisions became overwhelming.

By the end of 1933, Lillian was mentally and physically exhausted. Her blood pressure was particularly high, and after a two-month bout of illness, she reached a point where she did not have the strength to go on. During the time she was sick, the orphanage went deep into debt for the first time, and many of the vendors she bought food and supplies from refused to extend any more credit. Even prayer seemed like too much effort for Lillian as she contemplated what to do next.

One day as she knelt beside her bed crying, Lillian came to a conclusion. The children—all the children—would have to be sent away. Some had relatives or friends they could go to, and Lillian would beg other people to take the rest of the children in. She told herself that she could not stand one more day of the strain of running the orphanage. There were just too many needs, and she felt like she no longer even had the strength to trust God for help.

Wearily Lillian got to her feet and called one of the older girls. "Alya, will you please gather all the children in the courtyard and ask the widows to join them. I have an announcement to make."

"Yes, Mama," Alya replied with a surprised look before going off to obediently call everyone together.

When the children were all sitting neatly in rows, the smallest at the front and the tallest at the back, Lillian walked into the courtyard to speak to them. At first, when she opened her mouth, no sound came out. She cleared her throat and tried again. The children had to know her decision.

"My children, we are in a difficult situation," she began shakily. The usual fiddling stopped, and every child sat still. Lillian knew they had never heard her say those words before. She went on. "There hasn't been enough money lately, and there are so many of us to feed. Therefore, as much as I love you, I must—oh, I must—send you away. You will go to relatives if you have any, to friends if you have no relatives, and if you have no friends..." Lillian broke into a sob as she looked at the little faces she loved so dearly. Many of them did not have a single friend in the world outside the orphanage. "If you don't have any friends, well, we'll make friends for you."

There was a shocked silence as the children and widows took in what Lillian had just told them. She tried to smooth over her words. "My dear children, I will bring you back to be with me as soon as the Lord supplies our needs."

Then, as the children grasped what their Mama had said, they burst into tears, quietly at first, and then into a mighty sobbing. Lillian gave up her efforts to speak and joined them.

Suddenly a little boy near the back of the courtyard fell to his knees and cried out at the top of his voice, "Lord, Lord." Even from her spot at the front, Lillian could hear him clearly as he prayed. "Lord, I won't ever do anything bad ever again. Please let us stay, please, please."

Another child fell to his knees and then another and another. Within a minute all the children were kneeling on the well-worn paving stones. Lillian could hardly bear to watch them. They were doing exactly what they had seen her do so many times when they were in great need.

As the children wept and prayed, Lillian wondered what she should do next. She wasn't sure, so she got down on her knees, too, and prayed, "Lord, what now?"

After several minutes a calm came over her. She knew what to do. With a fresh determination, Lillian got to her feet and motioned the children to be quiet.

"I cannot send you away," she confessed. "We are a family. If we do without, we will do without together. We all need to keep praying that God will meet our needs. Perhaps it is good that you, too, know that we live by faith, that God will provide our needs if we ask Him."

Lillian watched as the children danced around hugging each other. "We are not leaving!" they shouted. "God will supply our needs!"

That evening Lillian went to the kitchen to see what was left to feed everyone. She refused to allow her spirits to plummet when she learned there were only a few loaves of bread and ten pounds of rice left.

"Cook the rice with lots of water, Mai," she instructed the widow in charge of food. "And cut each slice of bread into quarters. Each child can have some rice, some of the water it was cooked in, and a quarter of a slice of bread. The babies can have milk from the cow."

"And what about you, Mama?" Mai asked.

Lillian shrugged her shoulders. "I will be fine. Give the food to the children."

"But you haven't eaten since yesterday morning," Mai countered.

Lillian looked away. How could she eat when her children were hungry?

"That's all right," she said. "Let's hope the children's prayers are answered and tomorrow is a better day."

Chapter 15

Holes in the Desert

Lillian awoke the next morning with a feeling of dread. There was no food or money in the orphanage, and although she had told the children they could stay, she did not have the strength to hold on to her faith in the situation. She went about the day's work hardly knowing what she was doing. By lunchtime no food had arrived, so Lillian sent one of the boys to the post office in Assiout.

All the children gathered at the gate to wait for the boy's return. Lillian waited with them. It was no use pretending that she was not in desperate need of a letter containing money. When the boy returned, he handed her the mail. Lillian sifted through the usual bills until she found one personal letter from the United States. With trembling hands she opened it.

"Thank God!" Lillian yelled after a moment. "Children, your prayers have been answered."

"What is it, Mama?" they asked.

Lillian held up a check for one thousand dollars. When the cheers had died down, she looked at the envelope to see who had sent the check. A chill ran down her spine as she read the address on the front: Miss Lillian Trasher, Assiout, India. *India!* Then Lillian read the postmark. The letter had been sent directly to Egypt even though it had been addressed to India. How could that happen? It could mean only one thing: someone in the post office in Kansas, where the letter was mailed, had read the address, knew that Lillian actually lived in Egypt, and had rerouted the letter to her. *How astonishing! God is faithful,* she told herself. *Especially since we needed the check now and not a day later.*

That afternoon the children cheered as Mama brought sacks of wheat, beans, onions, and rice home for them. A steer was delivered as well, and the orphanage family ate like kings that night. Of course, Lillian knew that the thousand dollars would last only three days, maybe five if she was extra careful with it and put off several necessary purchases. For now, it was enough. Three days ahead without a crisis was a luxury for Lillian's tired mind.

Other money began to flow in. Lord Maclay sent a check for five hundred pounds, and a woman in South Africa sent half of her monthly wages. A local woman sent five dollars to buy the children fruit, and a post office worker slipped Lillian a week's earnings. One way or another, the children were fed, and the thought of sending them away vanished.

Although Lillian was often tired, she no longer felt defeated, and she became bolder about asking the members of the Assemblies of God in the United States to pray for her specific needs. In November 1935 she sat down to write a letter to them all.

> How I need your prayers. These children are just like any other children. Some are ill, some good, some easy to manage, while others give me much trouble and many heartaches. But all must be taught and cared for. The good mothers of America think they have their hands full if they have four or five little ones to care for, with the father to see about the money matters; but I have nearly a thousand and must do both a mother and father's work for all of these. And I must write hundreds of letters each week. Then I must oversee or do all the work. How I love my work and thank God that He chose me and not someone else, but I am so tired... Please pray.

Lillian also told them in the letter about another "faith" orphanage.

One of my boys who I raised from a 6-month-old baby is now a young man of 23 years of age. He has gone to assist Mr. Makiel Saleeb in the town of Souhag. Mr. Makiel used to be one of our teachers at the orphanage. About 6 years ago the Lord called him to open an orphanage in Souhag—a faith orphanage—and it is really wonderful how the Lord is blessing it. He now has more than 70 children and a very nice building, and he is the only Egyptian who has a faith orphanage in all of Egypt.

As Lillian wrote about this orphanage, she thought about how her life was part of a chain. As a young woman thirty years before, she had gone to help Mattie Perry with her faith orphanage in North Carolina. Then she had started her own orphanage in Egypt, and now one of her boys had gone to assist in still another faith orphanage.

The following year Lillian once again felt she was part of a chain that God was linking around the world. This time it was to an orphanage in Scotland. Lord Maclay had kept in touch with Lillian through the years, and in February 1936 he telegraphed her to say that he and his daughter would be paying a short visit to Cairo the following month. He would not have time to visit her in Assiout, but he asked Lillian if she could visit him in Cairo. Lillian made the arrangements and set off.

Lord Maclay arranged for Lillian to stay in a hotel in Cairo, and the three of them met for dinner. Lillian brought out photos of the children Lord Maclay had met on his visit to the orphanage. He studied them intently. Then he said, "Miss Trasher, you have no idea what it has meant to me seeing your work. After I visited your orphanage, I went back to Scotland and opened a home for tiny infants, and there are now thirty babies in the home."

Lillian's heart skipped with joy. How amazing: thirty babies in Scotland were safe and cared for as a result of her work in Egypt.

Lord Maclay was not finished, however, with what he had to say. "But enough about my life. Miss Trasher, is there anything your orphanage really needs?"

Lillian thought for a moment. They needed so many things, but what was the most important? Winter was coming, and everyone would need new winter clothes, but so far no money had come in for them.

"We could do with fabric to make winter clothes," she replied.

"Anything else?" Lord Maclay asked.

"We always need cows and meat and other food staples," Lillian said.

"In that case, I am going to give you five thousand pounds."

Lillian heard the words "five thousand pounds" and immediately began translating it into things: bolts of fabric, sacks of onions, beans, beef, flour!

She could see the storerooms filled to overflowing and the children in new clothes for Christmas.

Lord Maclay's voice broke into her thoughts. "I am giving you this money with one condition. You must use some of it on yourself. Surely there is something you need as well."

Lillian opened her mouth to reply, but the words did not come out. Then she started to cry. She wished she could find the right words to thank Lord Maclay for his kindness.

An hour later Lord Maclay and his daughter were onboard a steamer bound for Scotland, and Lillian was on her way back to the orphanage. On the way she stopped in Assiout to buy a steer so that they could all have a feast. When Lillian returned, she took great delight in seeing the children eat as much as they wanted. It was not often that they were all able to go back for seconds.

The following morning a telegraph boy stood at the door. He handed Lillian a slip of paper, which she read three times. Then she fell to her knees and began sobbing. It was just too much. Lord Maclay had decided to give the orphanage another twenty thousand pounds. The money was waiting for Lillian to collect from the bank in Assiout.

Now that there were food and money for many days to come, Lillian took time off to rest. One of her doctor friends insisted she check herself into the local hospital for a full checkup. Lillian was not surprised to learn that she had a weak heart along with her high blood pressure, as she had been having chest pains and headaches for months. There were no effective medicines for these conditions—only plenty of rest, which seemed an impossibility for someone with as many responsibilities as Lillian.

As she lay in the hospital bed, thinking about the toll that being Mama to so many orphans had taken on her body, Lillian had no thoughts of self-pity. She knew she would have given more if she'd had any more to give. Her walk of faith in Egypt reminded her of the fable that Egyptian children learned at school. It was a story about a boy who had to cross a vast desert. There were no watering holes along the way, and so, whenever he needed a drink, he had to stop and dig a well with his bare hands. After he had dug several of these watering holes, his hands were cut and bloody, but he went on. When he finally got to the other side, he was completely worn out.

A month later this boy watched as another boy walked out of the desert. The second boy had taken the exact same route as the first boy, but he looked fresh and happy, skipping along with a huge bunch of flowers in his arms.

"How could you cross the desert and look so fresh and cool?" the first boy asked. "And where did you get those flowers? I didn't see a single one when I crossed just a month ago."

The second boy answered. "Oh, the way is beautiful. There are many small wells brimming with cool water along the way, and around each well there are flowers and shady bushes. It was easy to cross. Didn't you see them?"

The first boy looked down at his scarred hands and smiled. He knew that his own suffering had made the desert an easier place to cross for those who followed after him.

Like the first boy in the story, Lillian was content knowing that God had called her to dig holes in the desert and that many flowers would bloom as a result of her toil.

Lillian was released from the hospital and returned to her life's work at the orphanage. She helped some of the young men to start a grocery store in Assiout. The store became very successful and provided the men with a good income.

Other wonderful things were also happening. Lillian had a small cottage built for her, slightly south of the other orphanage buildings. Adjoining the cottage was a second cottage, the "baby house," where Lillian brought twenty-five of the most delicate babies and cared for them. The babies lay, sat, or crawled in the lovely garden that Lillian planted.

The older children were thrilled by the addition of a swimming pool! A large engine pumped water to irrigate the vegetable gardens, and Lillian decided it could be used to fill a swimming pool as well. She drew up plans so that the water was first pumped into one end of the pool and then pumped out the other end and onto the land. Because the water was always running, it was fresh and safe to swim in. A campaign was launched to teach the children to swim, and many of them were soon competent swimmers.

Then on September 27, 1937, Lillian Trasher celebrated her fiftieth birthday. By now the orphanage was again caring for over seven hundred children. And the needs were greater than ever. One meal of tomatoes and cabbage took 150 pounds of tomatoes and 100 cabbages. The tiniest treat, when multiplied seven hundred times, cost a lot of money. To give each child a 10-cent comb, a 5-cent cake of soap, and a 25-cent towel cost Lillian 280 dollars.

In 1938 a well-known American journalist went on a world tour to find Americans living overseas and write about what they were up to. In spring 1938 Lillian welcomed the writer to the orphanage. The man stayed for a week, interviewing the widows, playing with the children, and taking notes. Lillian took the time to answer all of his questions, and she thought he left with a favorable impression of the work at the orphanage. She had no idea just how impressed he was.

In 1939 an article appeared in *Reader's Digest* titled "Nile Mother." The opening sentence of the article read, "Egypt is a land of wonders, but to me its greatest is Miss Lillian Trasher." The article went on to tell of Lillian's work in the most glowing terms.

The results of the publicity were astonishing. Many people whom Lillian had never heard of sent money to the orphanage. And now nearly all the passengers on the tour boats on the Nile were eager to see the "famous" Nile mother and her orphans. Lillian was a little embarrassed at being called the "greatest wonder in Egypt," but she appreciated the results of the publicity.

As the work of the orphanage went on, the mood in Egypt continued to turn against Christian missionaries. The government imposed import taxes on all churches and charitable work. A small tax would have been one thing, but the government wanted the recipient to pay taxes equal to the entire value of a package. Lillian's heart sank when she learned of this. It was no longer worth getting parcels of clothing, school supplies, or toys from overseas. Now she had to write to the faithful women of the Women's Missionary Council and tell them to stop sewing clothes for the children.

As the decade came to an end, the clouds of war that had been gathering on the horizon finally exploded into World War II. The Germans and their Axis partner, Italy, were eager to get their hands on the Suez Canal. In September 1940 the Italians, with two hundred thousand troops, invaded Egypt from Libya to the west and took up fortified positions at Sidi Barrani, about three hundred miles west of Alexandria. Just as before, American and British citizens were ordered to leave Egypt, but this time Lillian absolutely refused to go. She was now fifty-three years old and had lived in Egypt longer than she had in the United States. She felt like an Egyptian. Fortunately no one came this time to force Lillian to leave. But the path that lay ahead would be as difficult for the orphanage to endure as during World War I.

Chapter 16

A Shipload of Supplies

By 1941 the Allies had turned the war in Egypt around. The Italians had lost nine divisions in the fighting and were retreating to Libya. As a result of the war, many things, such as schoolbooks, cost three times as much as they had before the war, while other things, such as car tires, were virtually unobtainable.

The orphanage was now home to nine hundred children, and there was a constant need for food and clothing. By September 1941 many of the children's clothes were in tatters and the children were down to eating half a cup of lentils each for dinner. Lillian had done everything she could to get money for the orphanage, but it seemed hopeless. Everyone in Egypt was suffering.

One evening at supper, Lillian announced that all school and work were going to be suspended for twenty-four hours so that everyone could pray in earnest about the situation. As she visited the girls' dormitory that evening, Lillian was struck by the sincerity of the prayers. One little girl named Figa could be heard above all the other voices. Figa was not a pretty girl—her head had been shaved because of a skin disease—but when she raised her voice in prayer, Lillian thought it was the most beautiful sound she had ever heard. "Lord, You have said that when our mothers and fathers forsake us, You will take us up," Figa prayed. "We need You to provide for us right now because Mama says there is no one else who can help us."

Lillian tiptoed out of the dormitory room with tears in her eyes. *Surely*, she thought, *Figa is right. Unless God performs a miracle, we will starve.*

There was little sleep for Lillian that night. The children prayed until 2:30 A.M., and Lillian continued with some of the staff long after that. In the morning a telegram arrived. It read, "Miss Trasher, please visit me tomorrow for lunch. Ambassador Kirk."

Lillian stared at the telegram. Why did the American ambassador to Egypt want to see her, and at such short notice? Lillian could not think of a single reason. She just hoped it had something to do with all the widows' and children's prayers. Leaving her assistant in charge, Lillian took the midnight train to Cairo. She arrived at the ambassador's residence just before noon and was ushered straight in to meet him. The Honorable Alexander Kirk greeted Lillian warmly, and the two sat down to talk before lunch was served.

The ambassador was bursting with news. "I have something important to tell you," he began. "As I am sure you know, Greece has just fallen to the Germans."

"Yes, I had read that," Lillian replied, wondering what Greece could possibly have to do with her situation.

"As it happens, last week a Red Cross ship named the *Kassandra Louloudis,* carrying a load of relief supplies, was nearing Piraeus, Greece, when word came that Greece had fallen. The ship was ordered back to Alexandria to await further orders. Then it was feared that the ships in the harbor at Alexandria would be attacked, and the *Kassandra Louloudis* was ordered to dump its cargo and head out to sea under cover of darkness. A young Scottish sailor aboard the ship begged the captain to unload the cargo rather than dump it at sea. He told the captain about your orphanage. Apparently the man had given money to your work before, and his mother prays each day for your orphans. At first the captain resisted. He wanted to get under way, but the sailor was insistent. He assured the captain that they could unload the ship and still make it out of port before the sun came up. Eventually the captain relented, and the ship was quickly unloaded. The supplies are now in a waterfront warehouse in

Alexandria. Tell me, Miss Trasher, do you have a need for food and clothing at this time?"

Lillian let out a gasp. Had the ambassador just offered her a shipload of supplies? She had to be sure. "What did you say?" she asked.

The ambassador smiled. "I thought you might be in need. As soon as lunch is over, I will take you to Alexandria to see them."

This was one time Lillian wished she could skip lunch altogether. Supplies were waiting for her! She could hardly wait to see what was in the warehouse.

Two hours later, Lillian, Ambassador Kirk, and a Red Cross representative were standing side by side looking at crate after crate of supplies. The crates stretched on farther than Lillian could see.

"How much is here?" Lillian asked incredulously.

The Red Cross representative pulled out a paper and began reading. "Two thousand six hundred dresses. Nineteen hundred handmade sweaters. One thousand nine hundred pairs of boys' pants. Three thousand eight hundred blankets. Eleven hundred towels. Seven hundred kegs of powdered milk. One thousand two hundred sacks of rice...."

Lillian could not take in another number. She burst into tears.

When Lillian had recovered, the Red Cross worker continued the inventory and asked Lillian which things she would like to take with her right away. Suddenly Lillian felt a thud in her stomach. It was wonderful to have all of these items, but there was not a dollar left at the orphanage. How was she going to get them all back to Assiout?

Ambassador Kirk interrupted her thoughts. "Miss Trasher," he said, "it would be my privilege to pay all of the delivery costs. We will send the supplies you need immediately by truck, and the rest can go by train. How would that be?"

Lillian wiped her eyes and smiled. "Thank you," she said.

That night Lillian was on the train back to Assiout, but how different circumstances were compared to the train ride the evening before. She could hardly wait to tell the children that their prayers had been answered in such a wonderful way. A shipload of supplies was headed their way.

On Friday morning Lillian gathered everyone together and told them the great news. They had just finished cheering when a convoy of trucks began passing through the orphanage gates. More cheers went up. Hundreds of eager hands lifted crates, bags, and kegs off what seemed like an endless procession of trucks.

It was after lunch before all of the trucks were unloaded. The children all stood around waiting to open the containers. Lillian said a prayer of thanks and pried open the first box. It was filled with dresses.

"Let's start with one each," she instructed, "though there will be enough for two later on."

All afternoon and into the evening, Lillian and the widows gave out clothing and dispatched food to the kitchen. How wonderful it was to see the children glowing with pride in their colorful new outfits.

The delivery of the Red Cross supplies was a high point of the war and one that Lillian would thank God for many times. In fact, in 1945, when the Second World War ended, most of the children were still wearing clothes from the *Kassandra Louloudis*.

During the war years the number of children at the orphanage had increased, but with the war behind them, Lillian was confident that better days were ahead—that is, until September 1947, when another form of horror settled over Egypt: a cholera epidemic.

The epidemic initially hit the biggest cities, and at first a hundred and then a thousand deaths a week took place in Alexandria and Cairo. Slowly the cholera seeped out into the countryside, claiming thousands more lives. Death came within hours of the victim's realizing he had the disease, and entire families who had appeared healthy one morning were all dead and buried by the following day.

The government ordered all schools to be closed down, except for Lillian's school. Since the children lived together on the school grounds anyway, they had the same amount of contact with each other whether they attended school or not.

Lillian refused to think about what would happen if one of her children did catch the disease. With so many people packed into such a small space, the cholera was bound to spread like wildfire.

With reports that cholera was creeping closer to Assiout, Lillian prayed constantly that it would not make its way inside the orphanage walls. People were told to have as little personal contact as they could with other people, but that was not possible in the orphanage, which had a constant stream of visitors, deliverymen, and helpers.

Still, Lillian wondered what she could do to lessen the chances of contact with the deadly disease. Perhaps, she thought, she should not take in any new children until the epidemic was over. This idea made perfect sense from a medical perspective, but the thought of turning away a child—any child—in need bothered Lillian. It was something the orphanage had never done, not even during the Egyptian uprisings or the Great Depression. Lillian did not know what was the right thing to do.

One Saturday in October Lillian was on her way back from Assiout when she noticed a soldier standing guard beside a house. Her heart skipped a beat as she realized the door he was guarding had a white circle painted on it, the symbol of cholera. The epidemic had finally reached Assiout. In a panic Lillian drove home as fast as she could, locking the gates firmly behind her.

That night she read the Bible story about Moses and Pharaoh and the plagues, and she repeated the verse, "Neither shall any plague come nigh thy dwelling," to herself. "I will take that as a promise, Lord," she prayed. "Even if cholera is all around us, I am going to trust You to keep all the children safe. I will not turn away children who need a home, even if they come from cholera-infected areas."

Three days later Lillian's mind was on another disaster that was totally unrelated to the epidemic. It was around midnight, and Lillian had just fallen into bed after one of her usual exhausting days. She was nodding off to sleep when she became aware of an eerie light in her bedroom. *Strange,* she thought, *something is making that light.* But she was too close to falling asleep to question what that something might be.

Ten minutes later Lillian was awakened by the sound of the school bell. Now her room was filled with an orange glow. Lillian rushed to the window and cried out. The boys' dormitory was on fire!

The flames rose three stories into the air. Lillian ran for the telephone and called the fire department. Then she threw on a robe and shoes and ran outside and toward the burning building. The whole time her mind was racing; she could not lose even one of her boys. Many of the "big" boys were standing outside watching the flames, and Lillian ran toward them. Lillian's assistant Mena was trying to calm them down.

"What about the little boys?" Lillian yelled at Mena. "We have to go in and get them."

Panic gripped Lillian as she sprinted toward the burning building. She was almost there when she felt something clamp on her arm. It was Mena.

"Mama. It's all right," he yelled. "There were forty boys in the building, and they're all out. They are in the west courtyard."

"Are you sure?" Lillian asked. "Absolutely sure?"

"Yes, Mama," Mena replied. "I counted them myself. They all followed the fire drill we have practiced."

Relief surged through Lillian's body. A building could be replaced, but each of her children was priceless.

Lillian looked toward the bridge. Where was the fire truck from Assiout? It should be here by now. Just then Lillian remembered the 150 new buckets she had bought at a bargain price from the army. She raced to the storeroom and ordered one of the boys to break down the door.

"Quickly," she shouted, grabbing for the buckets. "Form a water bucket brigade from the pump to the building."

Hundreds of eager hands joined in, and within twenty minutes the fire appeared to be under control—that is, until flames began licking up the wall of the kitchen.

"To the kitchen!" Lillian yelled at the boys who were at the head of the bucket brigade.

In one chilling moment Lillian realized that the kerosene tanks used to heat the water were in the kitchen. If the fire reached them, a terrible explosion would occur that could kill some of them. Frantically she searched the road for signs of the fire truck, but the road was empty. She looked back at the fire. Her boys were covered from head to foot in soot. They were straining to douse the flames, but the flames were growing bigger with each passing moment. Overcome with fear, Lillian fell to her knees. "Do something, Lord," she begged. "The kerosene tanks are inside. Do something."

Lillian stayed on her knees for a minute or two staring at the flames. *It's happening,* she marveled, *the flames are dying down.* Sure enough, the fire fizzled out, leaving the inside of the kitchen unscathed.

Moments later the fire truck arrived. The firemen walked around the buildings and confirmed that the fire was out. As day broke, the ambulance from Assiout arrived to take the burn victims to the hospital. The ambulance driver could hardly believe that not a single person had been burned by the flames.

When the sun was fully up, Lillian and Mena examined the kerosene storage tanks they had been so worried about. The tanks stood untouched by the flames. Next Lillian and Mena looked at the wall, the outside of which had been alive with fire. A window in the wall was jammed open, and a wad of newspapers had been stuffed into the gap to keep the cold night air out. Lillian stared in disbelief at the window. She could see the burn marks where the flames had licked all the way up to the newspaper and then stopped!

"How incredible!" she told Mena. "I saw the flames on this wall, and that's what made me drop to my knees and pray. At that exact moment the flames must have stopped, or they would have consumed the newspaper and spread inside to the kerosene tanks."

"I think we are looking at a miracle, Mama," Mena replied. "How else can you explain newspapers that don't catch fire?"

Lillian bowed her head once again. Her children were all safe, the kitchen had not exploded, and they could begin repairs tomorrow. They spent the day cleaning up the rubble and relocating the forty boys to another dormitory.

The following morning Lillian heard someone banging at the gate. She sent her assistant Alya to see who it was. Alya reported back that it was a father and two boys about four and six years old. The boys' mother had died, and the man wanted to leave his sons at the orphanage.

Lillian sighed. "We just can't take the risk—no more children will be accepted until the epidemic is over," she told Alya.

Alya's eyes grew wide. "But they have walked for four days to get here..."

Lillian held up her hand. "It's for the sake of all the children. And besides, where would they sleep? With the fire, the boys' part of the orphanage is more overcrowded than ever," she said.

"Yes, Mama," Alya replied. "I will tell them. Can I give them some bread for the journey home?"

"Of course," Lillian said.

Alya left the room. Lillian stood alone, her words "no more children will be accepted" echoed in her head. How harsh the words sounded, how foreign. Lillian had never uttered those words before. She ran through the reasons why the boys should not come into the orphanage. They might be sick. But any child might be sick. If a Christian orphanage turned away a child when he was most in need of kindness, where would that child go? The father had walked for four days hoping that there would be a place for his sons in the orphanage. Now Lillian had sent word to him that there was no place in God's house for the boys.

Suddenly Lillian put her hand to her mouth. "What have I done!" she exclaimed. "God, forgive me." Then she raced down the hall and out the door calling, "Alya! Wait! Alya!"

By now Alya was at the main gate. Lillian ran up behind her. Alya was talking to a very thin, wiry man. The two little boys stood shyly behind him.

"Welcome," Lillian said to the man, holding out her hands in greeting. "Welcome to God's house. Come and eat, and then we will find a place for your boys."

All day Lillian prayed that she had done the right thing. She wrestled with the possibility of exposing the other children to the risk of cholera. Thankfully, the day went smoothly, and the little boys, Musa and Ibrahim, ate heartily and ran around with the other children. Around midnight that night, however, Alya came to fetch Lillian. As soon as Lillian saw her face, she knew something was wrong with the little boys.

"It's Musa, Mama," Alya gasped. "He's very sick. He has diarrhea, and he's vomiting."

"Does he have a temperature?" Lillian asked.

Alya nodded. "One hundred and five."

Vomiting, diarrhea, and high temperature were the symptoms of cholera!

"God, what have I done?" Lillian wailed. "Help me to do the right thing now." She pulled on her shoes. "Alya, call the doctor. I'm going over to see Musa."

Without a thought for her own safety, Lillian ran across the courtyard toward the boys' building. When she got there, she found two of the "big" girls bending over a bed, changing Musa's vomit-covered sheets. Lillian shuddered. If it was cholera, the girls had already been exposed to the deadly disease.

"Don't touch them," Lillian said quietly. "Let me do it. You girls step back."

Lillian took one look at Musa and prayed. "Help me, Lord. I'm sorry if I did the wrong thing bringing this little one into our home, but I couldn't turn him away. Help me now."

Within half an hour, a doctor from the American hospital arrived and confirmed Lillian's worst fears. Musa had brought cholera to the orphanage. Hundreds of lives were now at risk.

Chapter 17

"I Stayed with the Work God Gave Me to Do"

Lillian watched silently as a workman painted a white circle on the door of the orphanage. Musa was taken to an isolation ward at the hospital, but he died within hours. The health department arrived at the orphanage and fumigated the entire boys' building, and Lillian and the older girls scrubbed and disinfected the dormitory portion. Ibrahim, Musa's brother, was isolated. Lillian prayed and watched for signs that he, too, might come down with the disease, but he did not contract it. Despite the fact that cholera was highly contagious and that Musa had mixed freely with the other children, none of them came down with the illness.

The cholera epidemic had swept around the orphanage, but apart from Musa, not one child was infected. Once again, Lillian expressed her thanks to God for watching over them all. It took another six months before the cholera epidemic subsided in Egypt and life returned to normal.

The next few years were an incredible time of expansion for the orphanage. A small hospital, with an isolation unit, was built. A man from Philadelphia donated enough money to erect a beautiful church that seated one thousand people. New dormitories were added along with a bigger barn to house the twenty-five milking cows the orphanage now owned. Best yet, as far as the children were concerned, was the huge, new swimming pool that Maurice Doss Bey, a wealthy Egyptian, had donated.

The governor of the province came to visit the orphanage and wrote in the visitor book, "I received a shock of surprise today while visiting Lillian's orphanage. It is the most enormous thing of this kind that I have ever seen. Possibly her success could be written in three words: Faith, Faithfulness, Patience."

In 1953 the prime minister of Egypt, Mohammed Nagio, came to visit. He wrote, "Nothing has ever given me more pleasure than what I have seen today. It is as though I were dreaming of a paradise of humanity, exactly as I have always imagined it to be. It today has become a realization." Soon after his visit, the governor declared an annual "Lillian Trasher Day," where local merchants were encouraged to make donations to the orphanage.

As exciting as these additions and the public recognition were, Lillian never lost sight of her goal. It was not to build bigger and better buildings but to give the poorest children the opportunity to grow and flourish in a Christian family environment.

Nothing made Lillian happier than to spend time with her grown children and their children. On one trip to Cairo, she spent a night with Faheem, one of her married "daughters." As word got around that Lillian was visiting, the house quickly filled to overflowing with young couples and their children. Tears sprang to Lillian's eyes as she looked around the room. There was William, the son of a blind man, who was now the principal of a fine school, and Philip, who was a professor in Alexandria. Zacher was there, too, proudly telling everyone that he had just graduated with a bachelor's degree from Cairo University. And there was Edward, who now designed airplanes. The list went on and on as Lillian surveyed the room. Every person present that day had a story to tell, and Lillian knew them all. Many of them also had children of their own, and hundreds of little boys named Trasher and girls named Lillian were spread all over Egypt.

When Lillian returned to Assiout, an Assemblies of God representative arrived to write her biography. Lillian was reluctant to talk about herself, but she was eager to talk about all the wonderful things God had done through the years. Finally the representative pinned Lillian down. "Tell me, what is the thing, greater than any other, you are trying to do in Egypt?" he asked.

Lillian thought for a moment. It was not the kind of question she was normally asked. Her thoughts went back to the crowded house in Cairo, and she replied, "For these forty years I have been trying to live in such a way as to pass something tangible to a new generation. I would like to pass on a disposition of Christian character. I live before these orphans every day the way I want them to live in their homes in the land of Egypt. I try to show them how to smile, even in the shadows. Every hour of the day and night I do my best to live before them the life I want them to live before their fellow men." She spread her hands out to emphasize what she was saying. "I try to transmit to them a *life*, to know that if they can trust God, everything will be all right. I do my best to teach them to have faith in God so that they will be able to face life with a heart of trust. I try to pass on to them a power, a power of prayer, a power with fellow men that they may teach others how to find the true way."

Not only was a biography of Lillian published, but also the Assemblies of God made a documentary about her life titled *The Nile Mother*. The documentary was a huge hit in the United States, and although Lillian was a little embarrassed to be featured so prominently, she appreciated the opportunity for thousands of people to learn about her work.

By 1956 the results of the documentary were astonishing. Money flowed into the orphanage as never before. As a result they were able to build a larger dining room and add a second story to the hospital. Best of all, as far as Lillian was concerned, they received automatic washing machines from America. A church in Baytown, Texas, donated the washing machines, and Lillian had electricity and hot water heaters installed in the baby-and-infants' laundry room, where the machines were placed. Finally a task that had taken a small army of widows all day, six days a week, to accomplish was greatly reduced.

Another building, the Herman-Sadlo Building, which was named after the co-producers of *The Nile Mother*, went up at a record pace. It was built to house over fifty one- and two-year-old children.

Late in 1956 another crisis enveloped Egypt. Newly elected president Gamal Abdel Nassar declared the Suez Canal Egyptian property. Then in October Israeli forces invaded the Sinai Peninsula, and Britain and France landed troops in Egypt to take back the Suez Canal. The whole country was in crisis. As Nassar sank forty ships in the canal to block it, the situation seemed to be spinning out of control until pressure from the United Nations brought about a cease-fire and all foreign troops withdrew from Egypt. In March 1957 the Suez Canal reopened, this time under the control of Egypt.

During this time there was one particular bright spot for Lillian. Her sister Jennie, who had visited Egypt from time to time, sold her property in California and returned permanently to work alongside her sister. This delighted Lillian—the two of them had started the orphanage together, and now they would grow old together serving in it.

In 1960 Lillian received a special invitation to return to the United States to attend a series of Assemblies of God Sunday-school conventions, the first of which would be held in Springfield, Missouri. Although she hated to leave her children, Lillian was glad for the opportunity to visit her friends in the United States for what she felt would be the last time. Besides, she was leaving the orphanage in the capable hands of George Assad, one of her orphan boys who was now grown and had become an ordained Assemblies of God minister.

This trip to the United States did not involve a sea voyage as her earlier trip had. Commercial airplanes now crossed the Atlantic Ocean, and Lillian was thrilled for the opportunity to ride in one. The plane trip was fast and exciting for Lillian, and in no time at all she found herself in Springfield. As usual, she was wearing a black dress and carried one small cardboard suitcase that was only half full.

The morning after her arrival, Lillian spoke to those attending the convention. She told simple stories about the children who had come to her years before and about what they were doing now. Her motherly pride shined through as she talked about them. At the end of her message, she challenged all those in attendance to make a start on what they felt God had told them to do and not to wait for all the pieces to fall into place first. She finished with an explanation of her now famous "three-brick rule." "Once you know it's God's will," she said, "get moving! At the orphanage we start a new building project as soon as we have three bricks to put on top of each other."

From Springfield Lillian flew to Houston, Texas. Philip Hogan, the foreign missions director for the Assemblies of God, accompanied her. That night she was shown to a fancy hotel room in the heart of Houston.

"Here you are, Miss Trasher. I hope you are comfortable," Philip said.

But as Lillian read the information posted on the back of the door, she felt anything but comfortable. The sign said that the room was costing the Assemblies of God eighteen dollars a night. *Eighteen dollars*, she thought as she sat on the end of the bed. *Just think what we could do at the orphanage with eighteen dollars!* Finally Lillian could stand it no longer. She phoned Philip in his room. "Please meet me in the lobby," she said.

A startled-looking Philip Hogan arrived downstairs to find Lillian standing with her suitcase and hat in hand.

"I can't sleep in that room," Lillian said.

"Why not?" Philip asked. "Is there something wrong with it? I can get you transferred to another one."

Lillian shook her head. "I looked at the door and I saw how much it costs, Brother Hogan. That money would buy the milk my children would need at the orphanage. I am sorry, but I can't spend one night in a bed that costs as much as the milk for my babies would cost."

"Are you sure?" Philip replied. "We want you to be comfortable."

"I am comfortable almost anywhere, but not in the lap of luxury," Lillian said.

Philip chuckled. "Very well, I have friends in town. Shall I call them and see if you can stay at their house?"

"Please do," Lillian said.

Lillian spent the rest of her time in the United States staying in Christian homes. No one made the "mistake" of booking her into a hotel again.

Near the end of her visit, Lillian began having dizzy spells, which a doctor confirmed were related to her high blood pressure. Lillian decided she should cut short the last week of her visit and return home to Assiout. Lillian's condition did not improve, however, and for several weeks after returning, her life hung in the balance.

Although her strength was limited, Lillian insisted on tending to the babies as best she could. She often sat in her rocking chair in the courtyard, where the children would surround her and proudly recite Bible verses to her or entertain her with their acrobatic tricks. On Sundays Lillian loved to sit in church and survey her children with a motherly pride. The children ranged in age from babies all the way to adults. George Assad, who had come to Lillian at six years of age, was now the orphanage pastor.

After church one day, a visitor asked Lillian if she ever got tired of her hard work. "Goodness, no!" seventy-four-year-old Lillian exclaimed with a smile. "What a great joy it is to take in a new baby. Even though it is dirty—no, really filthy!—thin, sick, and motherless, we receive it. We give it a warm bath and a bottle of milk. We put it in a nice, clean crib, where it gets its first untroubled, comfortable sleep. You see, my babies are not orphans to me; they are the dearest things I have in life. I pray for them and dream of them. When a ragged, dirty child is brought to me, I try to picture how he will look in eight or ten years if we do not take him in, and what he will be if we refuse him. That is why I don't dare refuse children. I thank God that we have never had to refuse any who really needed us. I have never been as happy as I am now in this work God has given me to do. I would not exchange what I have done and am doing for all the wealth of America. This *is* life, to help those who need you and those who have no one else but you."

Lillian's physical condition did not improve, and finally, in early October 1961, she was hospitalized in Assiout, where the doctors categorized her condition as grave.

On Sunday, December 17, 1961, two new babies were welcomed into the orphanage. That same day Lillian Trasher died. Jennie was at her side. Lillian had been in the Assiout hospital for ten weeks with heart problems. The doctors concluded that at seventy-four years of age, her body had simply worn itself out.

The funeral was a hastily organized affair because, according to Egyptian law, the body needed to be buried before nightfall. A horse-drawn carriage carried Lillian's body slowly through the streets of Assiout back to the orphanage. Both Christians and Muslims wept as Mama Lillian's casket passed. Stunned children lined up by the gateway in silence as they tried to grasp what had happened. A solemn ceremony was held in the huge orphanage church where Lillian had preached just weeks before. Lillian Trasher's body was buried in the orphanage cemetery, surrounded by the graves of several of the children whom she had loved so dearly.

For weeks after Lillian's death, her living children returned to Assiout to pay their respects at Mama's grave. Many wept as they recalled her love for them and her unwavering faith that God did indeed look after the widows and the orphans.

No one knows for sure exactly how many widows and children Lillian Trasher cared for, though the number was certainly close to ten thousand. Some of them stayed a brief time at the orphanage and others for a lifetime.

Thousands of people in the United States and around the world mourned Lillian's death. In the United States many articles were written about Lillian's remarkable life. One of them read, "Lillian Trasher, whom the press once described as the 'greatest American woman living outside the United States,' ranked high among the missionary heroines of her time. During her fifty years of orphanage work in Egypt, she cared for nearly ten thousand children, the homeless, the helpless, and the blind. They called her 'The Nile Mother.'"

One day, not long before she was hospitalized, a news reporter had asked Lillian, "Miss Trasher, what is the secret of your missionary success? What is the greatest thing you ever did?"

"There isn't any secret," Lillian answered quickly. "I just stayed! I did not quit. I stayed with the work God gave me to do."

Bibliography

Howell, Beth Prim. *Lady on a Donkey.* E. P. Dutton & Company, 1960.

Letters from Lillian. Assemblies of God, Division of Foreign Missions, 1983.

Sumrall, Lester. *Lillian Trasher: Nile Mother.* Gospel Publishing House, 1951.

Additional material from the archives of the Assemblies of God World Missions, Springfield, Missouri.

About the Authors

Janet and Geoff Benge are a husband and wife writing team with more than thirty years of writing experience. Janet is a former elementary school teacher. Geoff holds a degree in history. Originally from New Zealand, the Benges spent ten years serving with Youth With A Mission. They have two daughters, Laura and Shannon, and an adopted son, Lito. They make their home in the Orlando, Florida, area.

CHRISTIAN HEROES: THEN & NOW are available in paperback, e-book, and audiobook formats, with more coming soon!

www.YWAMpublishing.com